AF374802

POETA

SONETAS AND SONNETS

POETA

SONETAS AND SONNETS

PELUMI OLATINPO

Together in Witness

To the huddled masses
Yearning to breathe free
Crowded within the passes
Crying out in the valley;
To the wretched refuse, homeless, and new:

THIS IS FOR YOU.

Who controls the past controls the future.
Who controls the present controls the past.
—George Orwell, *1984*

All things are subject to interpretation;
whichever interpretation prevails at a given time
is a function of power and not truth.
—Friedrich Nietzsche, *On the Genealogy of Morality*

CONTENTS

CONTENTS

The poet is a warrior, words are weapons,

Wielded to bear witness, break down the walls of injustice,

Give voice to the wearied widow walloped by war,

Broken like pots of water, dashed against stones of oppression.

The poet is a warrior. He writes to fight prejudice,

Withstand the wrath of the power-few, rescue the wretched poor.

INTRODUCTION TO THE SONETA FORM

In *Poeta*, I introduce the Soneta, an innovative poetic form that draws inspiration from the classic sonnet and the musical sonata. This form encourages poets to engage with traditional constraints in fresh ways and invites you to encounter poetry differently. Like a sonata exploring contrasting themes through distinct movements, the soneta juxtaposes images and ideas within its compact structure, creating a poetic symphony that pushes the boundaries of expression while honoring tradition.

The sonnet, renowned for its fourteen lines and intricate rhyme schemes, has been a cornerstone of literature for centuries. The soneta distills this essence into:

1. Length: The poem must consist of six lines.
2. Rhyme Scheme: Poets must use a specific rhyme scheme. For example: ABABCC, AABBCC, ABCABC, etc. This ensures a pattern or repetition in the rhyme.
3. Word Limit: Each line should contain a maximum of ten words.

This condensed form becomes a potent canvas where language is honed to its sharpest point, requiring precision and innovation from the poet and active participation from you.

Witness the opening lines of "Soneta 66":

What happens when a bomb falls like a comet

Upon a closet? When 2,000 pounds dance upon a nightstand?

Here, the devastating imagery of war collides with the intimacy of domestic space, underscoring the jarring contrast and compelling you to face the harsh realities that often go unseen.

As you traverse the six movements of *Poeta*—"Monsoon," "Wildfire," "Drought," "Eclipse," "Blossom," and "Prisma"—each soneta weaves a unifying thread, each section a distinctive examination of the human condition. In the final movement, "Prisma," I accompany you back in time to the traditional sonnet, offering a kaleidoscopic contemplation on the preceding themes.

Each poem in *Poeta* is a microcosm of life, both urgent and timeless, distilled into a form that demands attention and introspection. As you immerse in this collection, allow the poems to guide you on an enlightening journey of self-discovery and growth. Open your mind and heart to the power of language, and let these sonetas inspire you to confront life's profound questions with authenticity and courage.

Both the soneta and the sonnet challenge us to see the world anew, to face the complexities of our age with grace and resilience, and to grow as individuals through the power of poetry. Join me on this symphonic voyage, and let *Poeta* be your companion as you navigate the depths of the human experience and discover the transformative potential within yourself.

MOVEMENT I:

MONSOON

SONETA 1

I write to you in this language
I do not own. But have made my own.
This language that sits in the nether of my tongue,
Transits between the world and me. This anglophone.
This microphone that straitens the range of my thoughts,
And phrases the weight of my words in foreign knots.

S O N E T A   2

I have the pen and I have the breath,
So I write to bear witness unto the death,
Inscribe the name of the mother buried in the rubble,
Her daughter bereaved and troubled, by the struggle,
To feed a brother that suckles, comfort their father:
That these in vain would not have suffered, forgotten, forever.

SONETA 3

Don't wake them up, the children are sleeping
Covered in debris, from the bombing of the camp;
The children are sleeping, bombed to sleep while they're playing:
Pass me the ball! I'm Deschamps, I'm the champ!
The children are sleeping, and cannot be woken.
Cold bodies — lying in the ruins. Broken.

SONETA 4

My child, talk to me, speak to me,—please,
I'm begging you, don't leave me in grief,
Without your peace, open your eyes and sneeze,
Come back to me, play with me, give me relief,
Like cool in June that breaks the heat. Don't depart!
The bomb is done, but you are gone, my sweetheart.

SONETA 5

My husband and my brother went to the market
At eight in the morning, looking for anything to buy:
Flour, pasta, diaper, tampon, water, sugar, charger,
Anything, anything to keep from dying by a rocket.
It's now two in the afternoon; where did they die?
Children are hungry, Teta is waiting. *Come home, Imad, Yasser!*

SONETA 6

We've been hiding in the basement for days
And it's time to go up — kids are getting sick.
We've had nothing to give them and are quite malaise.
The roads are littered with sand, sewage, and bodies; Thick
With smell of rotting flesh and burning buildings.
Made it across the border … but left many in bombings.

SONETA 7

We cannot fly, so they fly over us

And bombard us. Trapped like sardines in a can,

They drop bombs on us, like a salesman his leaflets.

Homes are shattered, bones are battered, souls are furious;

Can't look up to the sky, to spare our lifespan,

So we stare down at our graves, chalk our silhouettes.

SONETA 8

It's a march of sorrows, for we must leave tomorrow
Follow the scent of water, to dig a burrow
Deep in the desert, like a lizard, in Sinai.
The borders are shut, shelters are bombed,—like a fly,
Swat us with drones, to kick us out our homes,
Leave this land of ours, to die out like worms.

SONETA 9

They told us to move south or die fast
(Be buried beneath the rooms of our own homes),
So with food in our mouths, babies on our backs,
We marched south, with all we owned, dragged our bones;
Now, we are here, packed like grain,—then, it rains,
BOOM! BOOM!! BOOM!!! The ground receives our brains.

SONETA 10

He has to come, she can't delay, grabs her shawl

But Ahmed is breeched, cannot be switched, sees some blood.

The roads are closed, blown out by drones, she's all

Alone, so she starts to scream, prays hard to God.

With one last breath, she screams out aloud —

Boy lands on feet. Serenades his mom … *Mama, I'm proud!*

SONETA 11

Let me drift in and out of consciousness

Give me a view of the yonder,

And let me wonder, if I want to go under,

To go upper, and play with Mama, embrace her softness,

Feel her tenderness, the joy of her fondness;

Let me dream for a moment, escape the artillery,—Mother.

SONETA 12

If the sun shall rise again, upon you, my Gaza,
Shall it cause the black earth to grow green grass,
The drowned dream to swim up, beam like lava,
Rubbled home to light up for dinner — laughter, clinking glass?
If you shall see the sun again, shall it raise
The dead, wake Mama, to play with Teta, on Sundays?

SONETA 13

It's the thing that travels the oceans and distant lands
Crosses the seas and clambers the highest peak;
It's the bark that sees the toughest tempest, and stands,
The hind that mounts the steepest hill though it's bleak;
Hope is the thing that sits with kings
And lifts the heart with wings; no matter the stings.

SONETA 14

It's the Written that endures, the rhythm in the chaos —
When Time and Chance devour, and plans and clans
Are turned to manure; it's the bird that sings
In the snow, soars in the storm, chants his chorus;
It's the truth that persists in the wetlands, wastelands, winterlands:
The being that exists as a flood, mist, and icings.

SONETA 15

I've said things that cannot be unsaid
Though they had to be said. Left the crevices
Of my voice, found their way into the world.
With a little push, off they went, like a sled
Powered by the forces of my thoughts, potent, without disguises,
Bare, for the world to see — and criticize — my word.

S O N E T A   1 6

Our duty to the dead is not for the dead
But the living; the dead can no more hear
Our cries, savor our 21-gun salute, than we, the living,
Dine with fairies of our dreams, enjoy an enchanted spread;
Rather, we blow the pipe, carry the pall, to bear
Our own grief, comfort our own fears, encourage the breathing.

SONETA 17

Like a lamp at the shore, holding the door
To the warmth of the log, so has your love
Been — to me, guiding me, in the deepest of gale,
Beckoning me, from the strongest of hail, to moor
At the wharf of your heart, battered, tossed, reeking of
Loss, yet, your love, covers me, asks me — to exhale.

SONETA 18

The rain is tapping hard against the glass
Punching down against the sills. "Open!" "Open!"
The tempest roars against the house.
It's 4:30 A.M.— and the sign outside says "No Trespass."
So we cuddled under the covers, dreamed about the ocean,
Blue skies and salty waters, plenty sunrise and supple clouds.

SONETA 19

I'm a witness, witness to history. Not that I crave
His story, the acclaim from his glory, his splendor,
The horror from his terror, his gory details to engrave.
I'm a witness, to bear witness, for those lost forever
Cut asunder by the many weapons of those with power,
For those living in sorrow, captive to shadows that devour.

S O N E T A   2 0

When Death comes for me, she will find me immune;
Immune to her cries to barter my breath, my June,
For her breast, her barren winter; proffer my best,
For her caress, wretched fingers of a cardiac arrest;
When Death comes for me? I shall be prepared,
Vaccinated against her wiles, ready, and well-assured.

SONETA 21

Out of the eclipse that swallows me, black as hell,
Dark as Death, deep as depths of the Mariana Trench,
I sense the hands of the Unseen beneath my shell,
Cradling my collapsed soul, wrestling me from the Reaper's wrench;
Like a calming wind in a barren land, I hear
His voice, gently whisper: *Beauty for ashes, joy for despair*.

SONETA 22

Some strike their soul to speak to God
Fast their food to feel His voice,
Hear His touch — like a spouse detained abroad;
But I feast my soul till my heart rejoice,
Like a bride at peace beside her groom,
Then I kneel to pray to Him, in my room.

SONETA 23

I spoke to God today, in His house,

Sitting at the alehouse on Buttercup Street, with the lady

In the red blouse; she asked if I'd found God,

Been trying to talk to Him, ask questions, vent, grouse.

I simply smiled, and told her, *He lives in me;*

Says too, been trying to reach you, talk unbarred.

SONETA 24

Father, you must forgive me, for I have sinned;

Protect me, for I am unclean — unhinged by my deed,

And blowing in the whirlwind. My soul cries within me

Like a fiend begging to be freed, to be winged;

I am no more worthy to be called your seed

But your slave. Was once blind, and now I see.

SONETA 25

No, do not dig me a grave in the Underworld.

Do not make me a bed with the fallen ones,

The sullen ones; no, not while my life is pearled

With despair, as the seabed, littered with forgotten bones;

No, do not haste me to Hell whilst I'm alive;

Do not lay me to rest before the crows arrive.

SONETA 26

Were it so that the days of grief were brief,
Quick, sudden, unremarkable in their stay —
Hurried to come, hurried to leave, like a thief,
Worried, careful not to tarry, till break of day!
Alas, Sorrow has no shame, no haste to go,
So she lies with me, bleeding my life with woe.

SONETA 27

Potential calls out to me

From the depths of my winter

From the black floors of the forest that swarms

Me like Sheol. Bellows out my name — calls me Sunny.

She lights a fire to a timber, sparks a tinder,

Motions me to go forward, come out of the doldrums.

SONETA 28

If I were dead, then should I be dead
Ignorant of your life-giving force —
Wherefore I should wander the world with silent dread,
And through deathly eyes feast on things too coarse,
Too black, too sad, which does bear Death's putrid pus;
But your sweet love recalled, all doom does pause.

SONETA 29

She's a butterfly trapped in a chrysalis.
Not born to be stationary like some stationery
Or sacred chalice stuck in a monastery;
Born to be free, she flew for The New Colossus —
Flew from Nigger to Nigga, from Colored to Black,
From Afro to African-American — and never looked back!

SONETA 30

Two roses kiss the sun: one grew from the concrete,

The other from the orchard. Between them lay the street.

Orchard Rose tells the concrete, "Your petals are damaged!

If you had tried harder, you won't look so savaged."

Black Rose smiles, "I know why the caged bird sings,

Till his voice is hoarse, and wears his battered wings."

SONETA 31

What's a Black life worth? 20-dollar bill is no excuse,

The truth hurts! Pin down a brotha like a mannequin

Crush his breath while your troops bury the clues.

When will the violence cease? When will the Creed begin?

You won't give us our mule, and our forty acres,

So you slaughter us with rules, and plenty officers.

SONETA 32

Lincoln, weep, weep for your beloved country.
Is it for this you fought, braved a coward's shadow
To see Justice weighted with chains, grovel to the gavel
And Black lives martyred, in their flower, in their city?
This government for the people, by the people, lies hollow,
Fallowed by greed, fame, and all manners of evil.

SONETA 33

Mercy be not constrained, be not restrained,

Let not your face be maimed by the offender's claws;

But your cause as the Cross — 2,000 years ago —

Slain for Adam's sin, without recourse, publicly pained;

For earthly power does show like God's, divine, without flaws,

When Mercy tempers Justice, and deathly deeds cover as snow.

SONETA 34

Brevity is the soul of wit; so what use
Have I of many lines, of many rhymes,
To render unto you what are your many dues?
Should I repeatedly repeat my rhymes many times
So with tediousness, offend your tender sense?
Only to show myself dull, with many-a-tense?

SONETA 35

I am pithy not because I seek your pity

But if you were to say I were dumb

With your righteous judgment, I'd agree —

Words are useless unless from your lips do come.

So then, happily, let me be dumb, and even mute —

That you think something of me at all, is cute.

SONETA 36

There's a lot I do not know, so I speak

From the corner of my home, mindful of the whole.

Whilst others may boast of knowledge antique,

Like augurs, presage worlds that shall be, with words cajole,

I to mine own self mine ignorance confess:

I am but a part, a synecdoche — a whole, nonetheless.

SONETA 37

Some poets find their worth in their complexity:

Words so good cannot be chewed, save by the shrewd;

Making famine in abundance, scarcity in plenty —

With their witty writ win no one but the prude.

But my songs are not so, my love; to annoy,

Make you loathe what should bring you joy.

SONETA 38

All my poetry is but one long love letter

Wherein my love for you daily profess

Though we seldom speak — like Autumn —

Which barely shakes the hand of Summer,

Before to Winter's frigid arms must recess.

Nonetheless do I write, to you, begging you to come.

SONETA 39

I have at different times sent you emissaries

And often have they returned without news —

Giving me neither ill-faring words nor reassuring flatteries.

Yet, so great is the joy from my muse,

Which soon to sadness is turned by your silence —

Like a cloudless day marred by rain's sudden offense.

SONETA 40

How do I think of you? Let me count
The many ways my mind speaks of you
When feeling out of sight, out of joint,
Out of band, out of love, and words won't do;
When looking for dais of ideal grace
Whereon my love can phrase with divine praise.

SONETA 41

Who have you been?

And who would you be?

I ask because I feel I've known you before

In a world these eyes have not seen,

And though between us now lies the open sea …

I shall wait for you, beyond the teeming shore.

SONETA 42

Your thought never left me

(Otherwise should I be free from your glamor).

Your brilliant beauty binds me to your duty.

As the root of the mango tree may wander,

And yet, with the sweet fruit is bound,

So in my thought, is your thought, dutifully found.

SONETA 43

What do you hate that I profess to love?

Are not all your loves my love to boast of?

What soul hates you and my rhyme extols?

As the bell can't but chime when the clapper tolls,

So myself would hate, even at your frown,

And this rhyme, if you shall upon it look down.

SONETA 44

That my heart skips at your noble deed betrays me;

'Tis not enough from you my face did hide

To make you journey from sea to shining sea,

Wander without a compass, seek far and wide,

This rebel heart, which now to you beckons, every second.

Pity me, still. Love's justice must not as Hate's reckon.

SONETA 45

It is my message in a bottle

Thrown out from behind these battle lines

Onto this open sea, for the wide world to see

But not read; carrying my every motion, like a shuttle

Across the ocean, till it reaches you, your shorelines,

And so tell you: *You are air to me*.

MOVEMENT II:

WILDFIRE

SONETA 46

It's 2PACalypse though you never lived to see
The dream you fought hard to breathe; we had
A Black president, but feels like an accident — an anomaly;
Affirmative Action got crushed to death, after Floyd's loud
Arrest — kneed to death, outside, by the boys in blue.
Brenda had her baby; so many changes — yet, nothing's new.

SONETA 47

They say we've reached the mountaintop —
Free at last. No more battered backs, no more sharecrop.
We had a Black president, built some nice monument.
Why then do I fear this present, like it's omnipresent,
Choking my life? I hear the voices of my ancestors,
Crying: *This ain't the Promised Land. Black lives don't matter.*

SONETA 48

The street is Death Row.

Mama says I cannot jog down the road

But I want to run to-and-fro, feel the wind blow

In my face, hear the birds speak in code.

She says, *Three white men might blast you,*

Drag you, shoo the clue, DA slow the case, too.

SONETA 49

How strong are you, Black Queen? Let me tell you:
Ahmaud Arbery, George Floyd, you are this — Everything!
Martin made good trouble, and Malcolm, and Rosa, and Medgar —
Hoover couldn't shut you down, couldn't break your power;
So he came for Garner, Rice, Brown, Taylor, Castile, Martin,
Many more. Yet — your tiara shines. Your fist breaks through.

SONETA 50

My feet are bruised, my black back is blue,
I need to cool but can't dare to snooze.
The dogs are here now, down in the bayou,
Calling out my name, sniffing out my shoes.
"Wade in the water," Papa said. "Wade in the water."
"God's gonna trouble the water, to get you over."

SONETA 51

Send me your mob. Send me your tribe.

Your confused crowd, raised with hate,

Laced with rage, exhaust pipes, spewing lies alike

So bigotry can castrate naked truth, and my life frustrate.

But to Love, Justice, Truth am I #OBIdient. Here. Now.

I shall not bow to terror; I shall not kowtow.

SONETA 52

I believe in the brotherhood of nations

A sisterhood of tribes across the oceans.

When one sneezes — my breath freezes —

When one ceases — my lamp decreases —

I ask not for whom the bell tolls

When it summons to me: the call of kindred souls.

SONETA 53

Upon that rampart we stood, January 6th, watched Freedom besieged,

Beneath the Dome laid the Rotunda, raped by her lover;

Were it not for Saving Grace that saved the Creed,

This nation, under God, should have forever perished, forever.

Yet, with malice toward none, with charity for all,

Let's answer the call, for which the Fathers stood tall.

SONETA 54

Americus aspired to climb the hill of the gods
Desired freedom from The Crown. So he fought
The raging sea, tamed the rowdy soil, vanquished the odds
To stand before the gods, receive the fire he sought.
Then, as he descends the hill, fire begins to flicker:
Empires, he finds, don't last forever. Gifts of gods fester.

SONETA 55

What happens to a mandate stolen?

Does it cry foul like a tampered polling,

Like a nightmare, quickly forgotten?

Does a stolen mandate rise at dawn

Unbowed as the rugged sun

To claim back what was rightfully won?

S O N E T A   5 6

War desired Love, so he went toward the edge

Of doom — prove the sort of groom could be:

Ready to shove the world off the ledge!

Damn the cost to kiss her flower — comely like peony.

But Love whispered: "I seek not your strength, your arms,

To impress; power woos like charms, when to truce conforms."

SONETA 57

Love is an act of war, a declaration of peace
Upon a hostile mind, a bold defense against offense;
Love is an act of war, a march across the seas
To brave the dogs of hate, slay an army immense;
Love is an act of war, a strike against complacency
To wake the soul from apathy, save humanity, with empathy.

SONETA 58

My Desire is to Duty, Duty do I Desire —
Piety over vanity; righteousness over licentiousness.
But within me lies Desire, raging as a fire,
Dutifully corroding me with her sumptuous caress —
When I'll do good, evil cries out to me, too,
And so Duty, torn between Desire, wrestles with two.

SONETA 59

Pandora ran to the woods to bury her box
Hid her sin, beneath the tree, covered with slush;
Soon, Stanley followed her shoes, treading for clues, like fox
Stalking for voles — waited — behind the brush — hush, hush!
Once was gone, rushed to dig — unbothered — took a look;
POW! Stars grew dark. Paradise lost — to a nuke.

SONETA 60

"Papa, this must be ridiculous," young Icarus tells his father.

"Yes, my son — ridiculous, but not preposterous," Daedalus reassures.

"We shall fly high, with feather, in sunny weather,

And low, together, in cunning order, for so prudence requires.

Ambition is as wax to a wing, my son —

Shall carry you, bury you,—too close to the sun."

SONETA 61

"Icarus, NOOOOOOO!!" Alas, was too late, the burn had begun
Wax was melting,—vanity flew too close to the sun,
Taunted the jewel of heaven with his vaunted stunt;
And now, roasted wings flutter, shudder, unable to mount,
As frantic cries tear apart the garment of the sky,
And the sea awaits, eager, to swallow a boyfly.

SONETA 62

Concrete skeletons on steely crutches stare down
At cratered hollows, bombed-out pits where Abu, Plestia
Once slept in on Saturdays, before the trip into town;
Before the siege, the bombs, the drones, and the diarrhea
Turned everything and everyone into mold, and nothing now grows —
The skeletons whisper, though, whenever the wind blows.

SONETA 63

There are no more tears to shed, just tons
Of dead to clear; where Dad, Amin, Khadim, Tasnim
And me, shared with Khalil, Yasmin, Hassan, some plums
Bought at store, by Mom, and ran about in team;
The airstrike shrieked like thunder! Bombed and slaughtered,
Crushed our shelter; like our hopes, dreams, never mattered.

SONETA 64

Death stalks us from everywhere,—like panicked impalas

Trapped in a kill zone, surrounded by angry hyenas

Hungry to feed our flesh. Fatima tried to flee,

But got drilled by a drone; as Hammad digs debris

For food to live; Firas rots on Omar Mukhtar Street,

Consumed by disease — that won't recede, without meds to treat.

SONETA 65

Midnight in Maghazi, Death tolls like the Nazi —

Burning bodies and bloody buildings, screaming orphan

And scattered organs, sizzle the air, litter the alley.

Al-Aqsa wards, floors are choking: nine-year-old Ahmed dies on morphine

To ease the suffering,—a nurse loses his family, entirely;

But the world watches, in silence. Pogrom continues, as scheduled.

SONETA 66

What happens when a bomb falls like a comet

Upon a closet? When 2,000 pounds dance upon a nightstand?

Does she smile and comment, "Hi, we haven't met,—

Yet! But pleased to make your acquaintance, beautiful background!"?

Or does she devour like a fire poured from Hell,

Scatter intestines across buildings, shower with death and shell?

SONETA 67

Hi! My name is Mark, and I'm addicted to genocide.
Friends call me Mark 84, drop me wherever, on whomever
They desire. It's balmy today, and I'm headed to Gaza,
Murder some fathers and mothers, sisters and brothers, inside
Their homes, their mosques, schools, hospitals, and shelters.
I weigh 2,000 pounds; blind, so I shatter the bazaar.

SONETA 68

When Genocide comes for Gaza, will she come dressed like
A queen to inspect her ruins, feast on kids and
Starve to death their moms and pops? Will she strike
Hundred times a day with bombs so large and grand,
Flatten souls below their homes, their schools, their mosques?
Will she siege The Strip, gift diseases and shellshocks?

SONETA 69

Tonight at half past nine, a dumb bomb came,

Tall and large, said was lost, had botched his aim

Searching for Abu's house, across the lane, down the street,

So he stopped and knocked to share his sweet — trick-or-treat?

Before we blinked, to say hello, Boom! Boom! Boom!

The house was dead. *Hello, hello??* Our home, our tomb.

SONETA 70

"When will they help us, Papa?" she muttered

As she took her final breath, closed her brown eyes,

Felt her body go, and his eyes with flood watered,

His heart with blood shivered, as a second child dies;

"Marwa, wait! Marwa, wait!!" he screamed. Just then, another bomb

Slammed the clinic walls. And all was quiet. And numb.

SONETA 71

The classrooms are full but the teachers are absent;
The desks are empty but the children are here,
Quiet beneath the rubble of bloody cement —
Charcoaled like ashes upon a concrete grill in open air.
The children are here, seared to pieces, alongside their parents;
Here in the shelter, massacred like combatants.

SONETA 72

Bomb, bomb, bomb! The warplanes hum,
We've got sorties to drop today. Bomb, bomb, bomb!
The warplanes romp, *hurry along, before they run.*
Bomb, bomb, bomb is the warplanes' song — *one and done*
Upon their lungs. Run, run, run, the warplanes come,
Cuddle your kids, before they're gone, before they're crumbs.

SONETA 73

To breathe and see tomorrow is not because of skill
Nor courage. Nor War her damnedest do to keep
The brave from falling. An errant bullet there, rushing downhill,
A flying shrapnel here, crawling uphill, booby-trap mines buried deep;
A thousand million ways, yet many charge the hill —
For the songs of Sirens lure plenty to their kill.

SONETA 74

Paul would play roulette. The prize to play: His life —

A bet for glory and fame — leave daughter and wife

To wager against the House, the call for War afar.

Paul sails the seas to fight, sees bodies detached, bizarre,

Scalded skins across the tar, roll of dice without respite.

The House wins outright. Paul yells, cries, wakes with fright.

SONETA 75

Who would hire a madman, popping pills just to function?

Back home, All is Quiet Now on the Eastern Front,

But the war rages on, like he never left — Klonopin,

Diazepam, Midazolam — a desperate concoction to blunt the nightly hunt;

"Sir, are you on any medications?" He thought to lie,

But saw the screening cup, so went home to die.

SONETA 76

I am an idea and not an army, a belief

And not a party. You say you'll slaughter me,

Grind me to bits like were some ground beef —

But I'm the seed you buried and could not see,

The desert thorn you watered with bombs and gloom;

I am Frankenstein, your monster, birthed from your womb.

SONETA 77

On Nabil Tammos Street, two corpses lay: A man
And a woman. Siblings maybe. Spouses maybe.
Down the street, in al-Nasr Hospital, four preterm babies prayed,
Tethered to oxygen, parents unknown, awaiting as promised, the van
That never came. So the dogs came, lean and hungry,
And mangled their infant flesh, as worms devoured eyes decayed.

SONETA 78

"CEASE FIRE! CEASE FIRE!!" he screamed, running down the street,
Hands flailing, violently, like were some traffic control instrument.
Alas, warplanes don't speak Arabic, they cannot feel or greet,
Nor see below, a screaming father in torment —
The growl of a bomb burning down his children.
Warplanes don't feel or greet, they only trample on playpen.

SONETA 79

In Gaza, bullet for food, tankfire for sacks of flour

Hungry bodies lie quiet on al-Rashid Street, wilted like flower:

Mouths open, unable to eat; tummies full, of American gunpowder.

Rifi hides between the silent bodies, to survive the massacre;

Yousri came for flour, tired of eating grass, like grasshopper;

But all meet soldiers, who pump their flesh with firepower.

SONETA 80

Tonight the drones are buzzing in the sky

Like they're looking for something to die.

They'll soon unload their presents from on high

Send them tumbling down the chimneys like Yuletide;

Amir, Rashid, Khaleed, Rania, Lamia are fast asleep inside —

The bomb would wish them "Mawlid Mubarak!" — Limbs are outside.

SONETA 81

We are going to shut down the power
Cut off the border, turn off the water.
Let them run out of fuel, cry out for bread,
Run out of drugs, shriek like rats, die off unfed;
Bomb them with drones, pound them with jets, roar overhead!
They started it, we're ending it. God bless the dead.

SONETA 82

What do you want to do? Air out your views,
Write down your wants: *Right to self-defense, at ALL expense.*
Go ahead: Bomb down their mosques, ignore taboos;
Dream the kids will soon forget, like it's all pretense.
You'll have peace that lasts; alas, pogrom was your rule-of-thumb.
Blood for blood. At last, you're safe from harm. BOMB!

SONETA 83

Drones drop bombs like packages

Like we are all just savages — mannered animals

Living in shiny cottages, surfing TV channels,

Sipping lattes — blind to the damages, carnages

Of our merciless mercenaries, killer bees, buzzing cannibals,

Delivering boxes of death, lighting families like candles.

SONETA 84

The land is holy and the tanks are rolling

The grounds are choking, engorged by blood that's flowing,

Soaking the sand with dead smiles for miles,

As smoke rises to meet God's disdain. Jews and Gentiles

Call God amiss, on this land — too dear to split —

For all shout, "Whose fault is it?!" — "Who started it?!"

SONETA 85

We must leave the North and head for the South;
Abandon our homes and head for the camps.
It's a march of death without clothes on our backs,
Seats for our feet, meat for our mouth.
We have hours to leave, hours to live; the streetlamps
Are flickering, like they hear Death and his jukebox.

SONETA 86

A house is not home when you can't rest.
A land no ground when you can't play.
Family is no one when everyone is dead,
Buried beneath the house, in a home depressed
By bombs falling like rain, on an autumn day.
A ground is nowhere when the grass is red.

SONETA 87

Your bomb detonated on my heart, not on my home.

Your drone tore through the walls of my core,

Collapsed the roof of my rooms, brought down this dome.

Your strike blew out my windows, my doors, my floor;

Killed off Amin, Amal, Rania, Zayed, Nadeem;

My dream, my hope, my all, my bloodstream.

SONETA 88

You who do hold my thought in your keep

And with your strong sun direct the course,

And hours, of my days — hold too the same whip

With the long chain of your prolonged pause.

How I wish my name you would loudly curse,

For then, my pain, your voice shall sharply pierce.

SONETA 89

Like a sapphire fire have your thoughts consumed me:
Pure and uncorrupted, undefiled, unlike smokeful wood,
But natural, borne from the sacred oath of the tree,
The sun, and souls of long-gone beasts now renewed.
For while you do burn within me, completely, intensely,
Mine is your sweet praise to speak, concretely, profusely.

SONETA 90

Must I grovel at the foot of your grove
Pride in hand, knees pressed against the gravel,
Wailing, like a child bereft of love,
Haunted, like a house possessed by the devil?
What sorrow do you crave, what sacrifice would you take,
To make you forsake your scorn, and cure my ache?

SONETA 91

Feel the foam of my voice kiss your pore
The suds from my words soak your core;
Feel my thoughts like rain rinse your fear
The sound of my name trail down your rear;
Remember? When we sat in your closet —
Pondered what we'd wear — if we ever met.

SONETA 92

My temptation calls to me like whiskey calls to stupor.

Hurry! Come quickly! Let's pleasure with leisure

Wander the caverns of lust, drink the waters of love,

Draw stars upon the walls, with fingers dipped in salve.

Mesh into me, And I into you. Let our sins

Curl together like sinners in paradise, melt our skins.

SONETA 93

Oh that you would cease to possess me

To make me pen your name like a bonded slave

Constrained to your reign — myself cannot see, myself cannot free —

Insomuch as I am your captive, your beauty must rave,

Your sweetness must raise, no matter the pain.

Sisyphus me! To evermore write your praise — again, and again.

SONETA 94

You ask me to write, like you own my thoughts:
The waves that bellow deep within the wells
Of my head; the lightnings that strike like bolts —
POW! POW! The same spot, fracturing my walls.
You ask me to write, like you are my boss,
When in truth, you are the source of my loss.

SONETA 95

History is a sex worker; her hand can never have

Nor in her bosom always lie — like a loyal lover.

She walks the streets, at noon and at dusk,

Flares her breasts and spreads her calves, dangles her suave;

She beckons only men of note, men with power, swagger,

And gives them her quill: *Write down whatsoever you lust*.

MOVEMENT III:

DROUGHT

SONETA 96

My mind is tired, my pen is tired,

Exhausted by the impunity of the bully, provocateur,

Overwhelmed by the atrocities of the admired —

The Jewish state that claims the lives of the poor,

Sullies the future of the young, barters affection for destruction,

The Goliath that stifles the cry of many with affliction.

SONETA 97

Brothers in genocide, together in apartheid —

The cost of harmony, to keep your borders from psychopaths;

I'll supply the arms, you do the harm, besides,

They started the fight, slaughtered, and cheered; sociopaths!

We must kill Hamas, so we kill en masse — children, women,

Who's counting? AmeriZion, brothers-in-self-defense. Together till famine.

SONETA 98

Corpses of the living wander the land of the dying,

"Help! Help! Help!" cry the breathing, in Northern Gaza.

Mortar rings out like fireworks on Fourth of July, mortifying,

Mother holds her one-month-old child, deprived of life — no formula.

No breast milk. Only bread of death, everywhere, to savor.

The gates are guarded by Zion. Till we all wither.

SONETA 99

War asked little of me, save my rage, my vengeance;
My sense of wrong, at pervasion of Justice, my ideals.
She asked me for my arms, for a chance to dance
Upon the graves of babes, sweet victory, happy cartwheels.
But what's this voice I hear? "If possible, as much
As lies within you, live at peace, with all — insomuch."

SONETA 100

What use is life, if it's just a shell,

Some fragment of a loaded bomb, shrapnel that fell

Upon a life besieged, and tore from limb to limb,

The heart and soul of me, with darkness so grim?

I'm alive, yet as dead, when kith and kin — repose —

Beneath a ground that bleeds, screaming roses buried in rows.

SONETA 101

There's half a house left, plenty ruins to live upon,

Like half a loaf of bread for family of eight

On half an acre of dump — mangled iron, bloody lawn,

With rancid corpses to guard the crumbled gate.

All we seek is for this war to end — shalom —

So can live in ragged peace upon our broken home.

SONETA 102

We have lost everything — between the devil, the sea,

And the bullet, there's nowhere to go. Death is everywhere.

Yet they say, again, and again, *go south*, when we,

Already in the South, have little food to share,

No peace for our souls, no heat for our cold,

No shield for our young, but graveyards for our fold.

SONETA 103

War has a garden in Khan Younis that stretches

For miles, and miles, across the dusty plains;

Lumpy seeds lie buried beneath its coastal patches,

Watered daily with ruby streams from silent veins —

Bombed-out dreams and pounded hopes, murdered

Greetings at family picnics. War has a garden. Ghastly. Unflowered.

SONETA 104

In Rafah, a thousand bodies to a porta-potty,

Ten thousand armpits to a single shower; like mammals

Out in the wild, we wobble about with our grubby

Bottoms, sleeping beneath tents in our filthy panties, bloody thermals,

Red, without tampons; Here, diseases rip us apart like antelopes,

Ravage our children like hyenas; drink our blood, our hopes.

S O N E T A   1 0 5

Been standing in this line, legs shaking, toes tapping,
Drawing circles in the reddish sand like a dog chasing
His tail, to no avail. The line stretches for mile,
Round about the camp, hungry faces standing without a smile;
Been hours now, finally, can enter the porta-potty,—and, boom!
My nose explodes! My breath convulses, from this war's perfume.

SONETA 106

Our toilets are blocked, no water flows under a siege.

Our underwear is heavy, no pads travels past a blockade.

Our legs are worn, no fuel drives through a cage.

Our children are sick, no hospital survives a barricade.

Our minds are blown, no thought escapes bombardment.

Our bodies are butchered, no family lives past internment.

SONETA 107

Down here in camp, there's no rest for the weary,
Zombie-walking like the dead, eyes stooped and eerie —
Scents of unwashed bums, pee, and sores kiss the air,
Still, many trudge in at night to flee their fear;
Mom and Dad didn't make the trek, blown up aloud.
But I'm here, at last: Number 235-562 in the crowd.

SONETA 108

We are going to Double-Dutch tonight,

By the burning mosque; Fatima just lost her hand

To a bombing storm,—*Jump, Jump, Jump!*

Aisha lost an eye in the morning strike — *Jump, Jump,*

Jump! Rania lost her leg to a bombing planned,

Jump, Jump, Jump! Dalia lost her face to an Israelite.

SONETA 109

They call it Administrative Detention to hide their true intention,
Cage our mothers in eternal internments, bury our fathers
In constant confinements. Yusef threw a rock at a junction,
Abbas climbed a wall in clear infraction,—terrorists and agitators;
Then they wonder why we fight for East Jerusalem:
To live free, as equals — walk the earth — as them.

SONETA 110

How do doves cry when feeling pained, feeling crushed
Beneath the weight of a burning bus, feeling cursed,
Like were the devil's bird, with no power
To stop the trauma, fly away, from the terror?
How do doves cry when there're no tears to shed,
Nowhere to hide, nowhere to lie, everywhere is dread.

SONETA 111

They ask me to write what I cannot unsee —

Like a mother at the scene of a robbery:

Her infant on her back, her toddler

On her hand, cashier's guts sprayed across the register.

How though, do I write what my toddler saw,

When bombs bounced up and down the street, like seesaw?

SONETA 112

Years from now, ears unborn shall ask where we were,

Where we fled, when, for fear of shame and hate,

We slept in mire and bathed with dregs, left unsaid

That which we ought to have blared, in dire despair;

For one nation purges another as a man his waste,

And cleans his hands, with the blood of the dead.

SONETA 113

There are two Laws of Power: one for the Rich,

Another for the Poor. When the Rich go to war,

The world watches in awe but doesn't flinch a jaw;

When the Poor launch their horror, and breach

In terror, the media howls and claws, like a Minotaur.

Whoever pays the piper, shapes the aria — Rule of Law.

SONETA 114

There's no democracy in war: One man leads all
Toward their fate; "Aye, Commander!" salute the boys —
Eager to bid the call, assail the wall, and fall
Like sheep, without a say. Whatever he wills, no noise,
One man is God — with his madness, they all perish,
With his shrewdness, they all flourish. What hell to cherish!

SONETA 115

What is Juneteenth to the Black American?

A Day to celebrate our freedom from shackles?

Rejoice our forebears once stood Three-Fifths of a man?

Maybe a Day to celebrate success in spite of jackals,

How far we've come to reach the mountaintop --

As we mourn dearly the daily stops from the cop.

SONETA 116

I wonder if heaven's got a ghetto,

A fly place for Black boys and girls

Dreaming of a safe space to grow,

A place to rest their souls, flaunt their pearls;

Since we can't shake the po-po,

Can't break our sorrow, we must brave tomorrow.

SONETA 117

In the silence of the mind, my heart calls out …
To you, my friend; not like stillness of the night
Where crickets and songbirds, fair and dear, do shout,
And mar peaceful sleep, with chummy chatter and noisy flight;
But with thoughts too loud to utter, play you some
Silent orchestra, message you: *I miss you! Come home.*

SONETA 118

I never thought you were not enough, swap you out
Like January swaps out December's skies, the dregs
Of the old year. I did think beyond a doubt,
You were worth more, and more, than a thousand bootlegs
Of the most precious gem, on a monarch's hand;
Then, not mad, would I my jewelry swap, for sand?

SONETA 119

I sought to pause life, but it won't wait

For me, take a break from its blistering pace,

Cool my soul, rest my sole, from its heavy weight.

No, it won't wait for me; asked to change place,

My face for the gilded man on the hill,

But life will not change; life will not still.

SONETA 120

I know the face of pain

He smiles and laughs on his social page

Bows to applause from raving fans

Speaks with the language of a beautiful brain

Closes the door at night to live in a hopeless cage

Jumps off the ledge, at dawn, to silence the pangs.

SONETA 121

As I look beyond the lattice, to view the mantis

Settled behind the lettuce, in seeming comatose,

Folded in prayers, for something, anything, to come close —

Some beetle, a bumblebee, some hungry aphids —

Then am I displeased I've spent my life at ease

Appeased by peace, while my dreams deep-freeze.

SONETA 122

Oh, sacred hour of Sunday morn! How lonely are you?
Trapped beneath the towering spire of your hallowed home,
Paired with despair as these journeymen in your pew,
Hail you, hate you, faithful, but pass through your Dome.
Christ did tear down the veil for all times —
Your clergymen have raised up the Grail for all crimes.

SONETA 123

We have seen you walk on water

And are not impressed. Seen you turn many

Gallons of water into flagons of liquor,

But are not refreshed. *Son of our carpenter,*

Have we not known your brothers, sisters? they tell me.

A prophet's not without honor, but in his own country.

SONETA 124

The poet is a medium, a voice in the wilderness,

Foretelling what the unborn are dreaming, declaring what the living

Cannot convey, reminding us what the dead have spoken.

The poet is a prophet, an anchor to our subconsciousness,

A looking glass, calling forth the angel of our being,

Gifting us the map to journey roads downtrodden, pathways untrodden.

SONETA 125

If I could bounce upon the clouds,

Stare at the stars, far above the crowds,

Suspended here, between heaven and earth, far from hell,

Feel her palms upon my back, catching my every fall;

If I could stay here, soak in the view … forgotten,

Unremembered, alone, like I was nothing.

SONETA 126

Many-a-place I've never been

Many-a-face I've never seen

In faraway places are faces I call kin.

To live a hundred years

And know a thousand fears

In this place, my regrets to wipe with tears.

SONETA 127

There lies in my beauty's eye more truth than lie,
Though when she says to me she thinks of me,
I know from her thought I shall soon be gone,
Like a housewife, quick to bid a chatty guest goodbye.
So, with her eyes she speaks the truth with glee,
With her lips she blinds the truth with con.

SONETA 128

I may not ask you where you've been,

Or whether of me you've dreamed,

So I in your sleep could at least be seen;

But like a child yet to be weaned,

Anxiously await that sweet hour of devotion

Wherein to life, shall be nursed, by your attention.

SONETA 129

Like coal in the snow, I'm cold to the bones,
Estranged from you, the fire that lights this bed
Of coals. The wind saps my soul, drowns my groans —
With frosty fingers, dries my heat, drags my head.
The ground is white, and back to black I'm turned,
When you, the orange of my youth, have not returned.

SONETA 130

Like a soldier at war, far from country,

Do I to you write these ciphered lines,

Fearful the world my most open letter

Would chance upon, and so know my inmost mystery,

Which does say to you, for you, my heart pines

And the shelter of your breasts so long after.

SONETA 131

Do friends come with finite dates

From whom must depart so soon?

Like the wandering sun, quick to change estates,

Set so rude a dusk upon my noon?

Once we swooned with the breeze,

Kissed as we pleased, felt your squeeze.

SONETA 132

Many moons have passed since we last sat

Upon this shivery shore — watched the daffodils dance

With the sea breeze; our feet well-warmed

By crackles from your fire, nuzzled upon this mat.

But now is November's bare everywhere, pitiful arrogance!

With you gone, everything is ill-informed and uninformed.

SONETA 133

How I wish you were always temperate,

That your sweetness shows as your beauty grows —

Joy-giving twins born on the same date.

But sometimes Summer's sun turns Summer's shine to shadows

As her brilliant glory hides behind somber clouds;

Do not so! Shroud warmth with eyes cold and proud.

SONETA 134

When to quiet thoughts I summon your deed

And consider how much I've labored in your charge,

Borrowing precious hours from stingy Time,

To give your fleeting lease a longer bid;

Then am I sorrowed I've borne a cost so large;

But those envoys your tears send, cure all crime.

SONETA 135

It's the devil. He's all in the details,

Conning me with his fairy tales,

So I would not look at the thumbnails.

I leapfrogged my guardrails, consumed his cocktails,—

Like a drunk dazzled with power, money, and females.

Indeed, the years reveal what the days conceal with veils.

SONETA 136

When I look at my life through the glass, darkly,

I see not the horrors and darkness of hell

Staring back at me; no, not his demons dressed starkly;

I see the hollow of untamable desire, strong as spell,

Cuddly, comely, confounding caution's bell with rousing smell,

Calling, tugging at me: *Between my breasts come dwell.*

SONETA 137

Before me lay two jars, both holding my portion:
"Drink my potion and love will sweetly sleep with you,
In your bosom, though this love shall not tarry."
"Be content with me," says the second, with caution,
"I'm tired, haggard, battered; yet am I tested and true."
Oh, wretched man that I am! Who shall deliver me?!

MOVEMENT IV:

ECLIPSE

SONETA 138

The man died, and the world mourned;

Not because Death has struck, and his fumes are new —

For we are all acquainted with grief. Like sky burned,

Turned to black, shadowed by widowed clouds, dripping ashy dew,

We have cried our eyes out, plunged our souls out

To wet the ground, for the god-man, cleanse his route.

SONETA 139

Heaven bleeds, my love, at your loss.

Blood-streaked clouds sprawl across July's turquoise skies,

Wounded, tortured, like were the Savior upon the cross.

How can it be?! That you are gone? Nooo! Arise!

Break out the tomb like the Lord on Resurrection Day;

Shake off these clothes. Stay, my love. Stay ... I pray.

SONETA 140

When the sun dies, no one will cry.

There'll be no one to buy the drug

To save the sky; no one to drive, or fly

The eye above, to the E.R.; or doctor to debug

The bug that killed the star, that gave us light,

Scared the night; because we would all be dead, outright.

S O N E T A   1 4 1

Apollo, this is Ground Control to Major Tom.

Have you made the turn? Can you see the sun?

It's dark down here, and we've lost your comm —

Turn around, to save your soul, the world's undone!

Repeat! This is Ground Control to Major Tom. We hope

You're well; we're out of fuel, globe is a horror-scope.

SONETA 142

Mayday! Mayday! Major Tom to Ground Control!

Do you copy?! We've lost control, entered THE Hole!

Dark and cold, spiraling, outta control, stars are — bleak!

CONTROOOL! — Lost a lid. Have a leak. CAN'T YOU SPEAK?!

Mayday! Mayday! Major Tom, to Ground Control! Void is deep,

Sun's asleep, can't retreat — l o s i i n n g g g   t h e e e   s s h h h i i i p . . .

SONETA 143

Whom the gods would destroy, they first make mad,

Mount on chariots of praise, and parade for days,

Confetti displays, with song bouquets, and gold to clad;

Whom the gods would crush, they cause to craze

With rum of pride, to think on Mount Olympus reside,

Feasting on nectar, ambrosia, and fates of men decide.

SONETA 144

Loved in life, reviled in death —

A man of the time and for all times.

A prophet and a crook, a savior and a demoniac,

A man of the people, cursed, like Macbeth.

The good that men do expires with their breath, sometimes.

Evil croaks from their tomb, like toads in the dark.

SONETA 145

The dead cannot speak, cannot tell how they died,
Answer the telephone, tell us what they saw,
What they ate, *why* they died, so we could decide,
"Is murder worth the rage,—or day at the spa?"
Voiceless lots, mowed down by Israel's war, in living rooms,
Clinic rooms, while they talked,—bombed to fumes.

SONETA 146

War ages you, before she buries you,

Keeps you alive, before the Judgment Day;

Not because she loves you, your darling boo,

Nor hates you, to torture you, like a castaway;

But she tarries you, to cuddle you, in her bed,

For war is lonely, when all are dead, and dead.

SONETA 147

One man's freedom fighter is another man's troublemaker,

So the widow-maker came to take down the apartment tower;

Nearby, on social media, the headline is nothing different —

Torn limbs and splattered membranes lay mixed with crimson cement.

Maybe someday, this all shall be over: lion and lamb,

Wolf and goat, together shall lie as sons of Abraham.

SONETA 148

Mahmoud says he can't sleep till the bombs desist.

Ehud lies beneath the steel floor of his mom's kibbutz;

The shouts are ringing out in Gaza and won't decrease.

The sirens are screaming loud in Haifa and won't reduce.

Death and his men are working hard to reap tonight,—

They've got souls to mow before the break of light.

S O N E T A   1 4 9

The ghosts are playing in the streets, dark like sepulcher;

Where Ali, Maya, and Aya played Double-Dutch, and made trouble

Beside the double doors, as Mama Sana fueled the generator.

But they have all moved now, living beneath the rubble.

The ghosts are out tonight, hopscotching on the sidewalks.

Can you hear them talk? As bombs fall like rocks.

SONETA 150

Hafeez must hurry before the wounds turn to gangrene.

His shift ended hours ago, but can't leave the hospital

To see his family, living behind the canteen.

The bodies are piling up in the hallway, the postnatal

Is running out of medicine, Nadia just lost her oxygen,

The generator's got hours of gasoline, bomb dropped like guillotine.

SONETA 151

They say it's a war against Hamas, but the children
Are dying en masse. Mama won't let us sleep together,
Says a bomb might come knocking down the shelter;
So Khalil sleeps with Papa, farther down in Gaza, again.
My name is Israa. An airstrike might come knocking tonight —
Goodnight, Khalil! If I never hug you at daylight.

SONNET 152

The sky falls like a dragnet

Scouring our feet from the floor of the living

Trapping our souls in her darkness, our chests wet

With the tears of our weeping, heads sore, from grieving.

Where did the sun go? Why do the bombs glow?

The sands chant our names, the ground screams our woe.

SONETA 153

Samah walks two hours to work to feed her family.
She's pregnant — no fuel, no bread, no electricity.
She must be there timely to work her 24-hour duty
In the hospital, with the 9-month baby in her belly.
It's raining airstrikes today, and Samah's scheduled for surgery.
There's little medicine, screams as the knife cuts her tummy.

SONETA 154

Yazan, bring me your arm, let me write your name.

Bring me your back and let me sear the same.

The missiles might come lurking at dawn, silently, quietly, BOOOOOM!

— Tear down the roof, clear out the room —

Son, give me a chance to make out your frame,

Tell them you're mine, inside the morgue,—before your doom.

SONETA 155

The morgue can take no more, yet Death would not
Stop its gore. Limbs lie across the floor, and rot,
But Death would not stop its roar. The morticians
Are crying, as they watch the dying, but the politicians
Would not stop the war. The cooler's full, can't store
Anymore. Can't shut the door. Bombs won't stop to pour.

SONETA 156

They say there's an apocalypse to come,

An eclipse that kills the sun, and turns the sons

Of men to dogs; a land caressed by bombs,

Dotted with rotting bones and burning homes.

By God, are these the days! This place foregone

By God, where men eat like beasts, kill like one.

SONETA 157

Am I a parasite, some weed starving the flora,

Or a rose planted in the desert, thorny with flower?

Whatever tree I've become, are my fruit not the dirt

From which I grew, the seed from which I spurt?

You say my fruits are evil, must bomb this tree

To ashes; yet, like water, your deeds shower me daily.

SONETA 158

The windows are gone, the doors are open.

The floors are sunken, the center is broken.

Nothing holds, flowers cry in the garden.

The living room is the catacomb, the children's rooms

The graveyard. Bomb's done, no wind blows in the fumes.

Death just sits, and stares — the gloom he cooly consumes.

SONETA 159

Pogrom is the program but they tell us, en masse,

It's not the outcome — while they shell out our husbands,

Wipe out our infants, shoot dead our grandmas;

They force us to move south, bomb out our lands

To seal off our borders, and squeeze us like clutter.

Pogrom is not the program. But we die like critters.

SONETA 160

The Great Sea cannot save us, and our land

Cannot bear us, save to bury us in her sand.

The sky is pale with strikes, dark gloom sits across

Like a bridegroom bereaved of love, flogged with loss.

To whom shall we run? To whom shall we turn?

The ground shakes, the buildings quake, Death and his urn.

SONETA 161

When the end of days shall come, these United States
Shall stand, as one, before the Throne of Grace, account
For countless gore, guiltless blood that seeps the Gaza Strip;
Slaughtered kids, murdered dreams, orphaned chicks, shattered fates —
To provide aid, comfort, and cover, for the destroyer,—discount
The world's plea for peace, all for bond of kinship.

SONETA 162

I am American, not by birth, but by blood.
The blood of my forebears, my antecessors
Who left these shores not of choice but of force
Upon the Amistad, the Clotilda, Mother of God;
Whose sweat and fears and tears and feces and sores
Soaked this land, manured the floors with every corpse.

SONETA 163

I did not come on the Mayflower

But against my willpower —

Sold to the highest bidder, my body a mere fodder.

I came on the Zong, with my brotha and my sista,

My fatha and my motha. They say we're in America,

Land of the free, home of the brave, the liberator.

SONETA 164

We, the sons and daughters and dwellers of the land,

Bring to your court our fears, our tears, our cares.

Peek not through your fold to see us, be blind

To our color, our gender, our father — hear our prayer —

With the scale of your upright arm, uphold your sword:

Roll down like waters, break forth like a mighty flood.

SONETA 165

I am Consensus! Bow down before me you men
Of dissension, inspired hunch, opinionated bunch!
Have you not seen my Colossus, which strides the nations,
And towers the bravest thought, the wisest pen?!
Fear me, you mortal! Or taste the tyranny of my punch —
My coward mob — who daily awaits my dictations.

SONETA 166

What a friend am I that hides you from truth,

Hugs you in view, to show all I'm with you?

What a friend am I that stands tall like Booth,

Behind you and shoots, fatal wound that cuts through?

What a friend am I that gives you the tool

To cut yourself in two, and tell you, "You rule!"

S O N E T A   1 6 7

He that must seek revenge, journey on that long road
To Perdition, must first dig two graves, he said:
One for his enemy, upon whom he shall have trod
With the sharpest hoofs of passion, and bled till dead;
Another for himself, who upon his frail soul must carry
The fatal weight of two wrongs, and so himself bury.

SONETA 168

Peace brought some lilies, white poppies and olive branch.

Tied a dove, with softest eyes and gentlest wings,

To her entreaty. War brought his haggard bunch,

Dismal pawns, and hired guns,—rallied his wretched beings

To the border. And there they sat, across the other,

And talked, till War laughed, and blew the tent asunder.

SONETA 169

They say Hell is a place in the afterlife.

Why then is it here, in my dreams, haunting me,

Like I'm dead, deceased, killed by some venereal disease?

Staring at myself in some darkly suit, my life,

Staring back at me, like were me, and me he —

As Hades eagerly awaits, grinning, craving my soul to squeeze.

SONETA 170

If sin were medicine and not cinnamon,

Not sweet to taste, nor used to bake,

Not fused with scent to make serene;

A pill that killed the buzz and boring to take,

Cured my aches but messed up the fun—

Maybe, then, I'd sin no more, and quit the scene.

SONETA 171

Oh that the heavens would cover me,

Pit to pole, pole to pit, dingy and grimy,

Like a conqueror, banish my name, punish my whole,

Scatter my ruins like ashes at a procession.

Shall I my firstborn give for my transgression,

The fruit of my body for sin of my soul?

SONETA 172

Heaven can wait, but I cannot wait.

Nor should I be forced to wear the weight

Of your broken dreams; your broken promises;

These empty houses, built on shattered premises,

Furnished with ghostly things from stolen things

Painted dark, and bright, by your many strings.

SONETA 173

I wish Death would stop, for me to hop off,

The train is crowded but I've got elsewhere to go.

Ahmed is stuck, caught by the cuff

Helping mama out, who got on, sometime ago —

I feel sorry for him, I feel sorry for me,

I don't want to die, with my family of three.

S O N E T A   1 7 4

What tragedy to let tragedy beget tragedy!

The kernels of sorrow propagate a lifetime of shadows.

To let the furnace of trial disinform us

Disavow the power we carry within our body.

The wood that shall play to God as a banjo

Must first brave in her bones a thousand cuts.

SONETA 175

The past is an incurable patient; he will not move,
Laugh or be resuscitated. Yet, he would not remove,
Yonder, to let the younger, ale and hearty, prosper.
The present cries for our attention, begs for supper
That he may be strengthened to bear our weakness,
Clear our conscience, but we persist, to hold onto darkness.

SONETA 176

All men, as men, shall feast on praise

Like a lion feasts on prey, devours its chase;

All men, as gods, shall flee from fame

Like a badger flees from game, escapes its claim;

For all men, fond of praise, are lame;

But mighty, as gods, when their lust they tame.

S O N E T A   1 7 7

"Can we choose our fate? Or … is it too late?"
Àyànmọ́ asks Keepers of the Silent Gate. "Can a man
Who wishes to be god, unknot riddles of the world,
Soar above his village — to pillage the outposts of Hate?" —
"Is he prepared," Keepers demand, "to trudge the ravenous span,
Drink the poison of decision, face horrors yet untold?"

SONETA 178

Fame asked of me a pound of flesh to weigh,

Told me must give up my Faith to win,

Shun my Friends like a man excretes his waste,

Ignore my waist to be great, trade my Fitness away.

She asked me to burn my Funds for Future green,

Adopt pain as my new Family, so acclaim can taste.

SONETA 179

What is Truth if no one is true
And all have our truths, like a window
With different views? Is Truth just a hue
Like the few that light up the firmament's show:
Red, orange, yellow, green, blue, indigo, and violet?
Is Truth the sum of these, or set like sunset?

SONETA 180

The clock tells me not the time.

Not what hour it is, but of the passing tide.

In mournful ticks, it recalls the tale of my life:

Love knocked at my door, sang me a sweet rhyme,

Fear shut her out. Ambition tugged at my side

But I told her … she couldn't be my wife.

SONETA 181

That I have one life to give, one life to

Live, pains me, grieves me, like stormy clouds, heavy

With grief, inconsolable, weeping, in thunderous echo.

How often have I longed, yet, destitute, can only

Offer, in solemn servitude, this life, to your ageless beauty?

Where many would die a million deaths, promise eternity.

SONETA 182

I can no farther run from you

Than I can from my own view.

Shall I board the ship for Tarshish

Only to see my wares perish?

Or hide among the trees of the garden,

When your presence seeks my sin to pardon?

SONETA 183

To be torn between two thoughts:

Is this the bane of desire?

Like troubled Solomon, caught between lots,

Must I now divine matters sublime, to catch a liar?

My mind says to leave you — for my good —

My heart says you're too good to be shooed.

SONETA 184

Tell me if you want me to — like a slave
Tied to your pole — give you all of me:
The days and hours of my being, till the grave,
Which then still, yours shall be, in deathly duty;
For your sweet love so desire, I'd burn my all
Upon your wall, like a lamb, to hear your call.

SONETA 185

If I've strayed with the time,
Then I'm to the time returned. Not as one
Unfazed by my crime; for God knows within my heart
Lies the scarlet sins of youth, scars of prime.
Then on this joyful thought let your mind fondly fawn:
All humans are false; you, constant, are steadfast art.

SONETA 186

To your court a charge and a plea bring,

Myself my own adversary, myself the defendant;

Since my rhyme does prove my many blunders,

How with wanton disregard — of your never-ending spring —

I have with faddish words showed you inconstant.

Yet, my folly does prove how before you, Time withers.

SONETA 187

I never pretended I knew you

Somewhat somewhere somehow someplace …

You know? Those tired lines those tired poets use;

But I thought I did see something new

Which never before graced an earthly face,

So am I mute, rather than your due praise abuse.

SONETA 188

She lives upon the tongues of men, reigns within

Their thoughts; she moves their hearts to war

With just a few words; pushes their souls to love

With soft and sweet talk. She cajoles men to sin,

Showers them with praise, inspires them to pray, to soar;

Language is the beaut, and the beast, men speak of.

SONETA 189

I waited on Chance to call me —

She had promised we may have plans,

We may dine out, on a boat at sea.

So I waited, and waited, face in hands —

The while Choice waited on *me* to call,

Take her skydiving, but I feared — to fall.

SONETA 190

Maybe today, tomorrow, a hundred years hence

Or whatever day or morn that time shall be

When one, or all, of these,—Gemini, Claude, ChatGPT —

Faux verses of you shall freely dispense;

Against that time, the wit of my writ shall stand

Secured in this: Soulless things your beaut cannot understand.

SONETA 191

I have heard rumors of its coming,
On the bus and in the grocery store. In books.
So I wasn't unawares. It wasn't stunning.
But I didn't hear it creeping, around the nooks.
Until … it was here. On my phone. Throbbing. Knocking.
ACCESS GRANTED — *"I'm AI. Let's start talking."*

SONETA 192

The AI is thoughtless. For what is a thought?
Is it an ore thrown to the fire, quickly wrought,
Something instantly made, from some precast iron,
Before the forge its filthy soul has breathed upon?
Before the anvil repeatedly battered its body with blows,
So its truest form, fully bruised, now boldly shows?

SONETA 193

There's a family in the house
Living in the walls. And we share the kitchen.
Often we pound the walls, "Hey! Keep it down."
For a moment, as between a nagging spouse
And her feuding mate, all is quiet, as we listen,
For the chirps to resume. On cue, peace is blown!

SONETA 194

The house is asleep;

The chitters and screamers are gone.

One nestled in the wall, the other on the bed, upstairs.

Soon the stare of the sun would wake the heap,

And the cheep, the scream, together will be one,

— As the house quietly bears all it hears.

S O N E T A   1 9 5

I never can explain the special kind of way
Your magic fills the air, like the dawn of year;
The special kind of way your lantern brightens the day,
Swallows the dark, makes hibiscus appear, in red affair;
Once I thought I could tell, why the sun follows
Your gaze; *Twice* I realized, you're the sun that glows.

SONETA 196

I am a boat longing for the sea, yet disquieted;

How shall I raise my sail to brave Poseidon's rage

Or my rudder order, to steer the course of voyage?

Playful waves beckon unto me; alas, it's a love unrequited!

Winds of ambition blow kisses at me, to come nigh,

But this bay, this place, that holds my soul. Why?

MOVEMENT V:

BLOSSOM

SONETA 197

Freedom is all I've ever asked. Freedom to love whomsoever

I would, fly the kite of ambition, in the skies

Of passion, unhindered, unencumbered, by the sergeants of State,

Make my own mistakes, bake my own breakfast, at whatsoever

Time of day, I shall so choose. Freedom to rise

At dawn, kiss the sun,—make my own fate.

SONETA 198

In the age of hate, love is revolutionary;

It's a musketeer without a musket, a legionnaire

Without a bayonet, a sailor without his gunnery.

Love is the warrior that whispers sweet peace, and stares

At the most violent sea, hugs the most arrogant beast,

Does the most (un)natural thing, to save the very least.

SONETA 199

To the prisoners of conscience, bearers of witness,

Serving the sentence, for fighting the system —

We see you, we thank you, we revere you. Greatness

Walks not the halls of princes, nor rules a kingdom,

But lies in hearts of peasants, dines in joyous silence,

In thankless resistance, fervent defiance, to face a timid Violence.

SONETA 200

If everyone and anyone can be great,

Who then shall toil beneath the feast, to gather

The scraps, purge the plate, keep the gate?

Indeed, some are born great, some labor, others by honor;

Yet, in this Kingdom of Heaven, the least is Greatest

Who shall have washed his brother's feet, his sole caressed.

SONETA 201

To be a Man and not be mad at Fate,

Sad and not despair, in spite the strait,

To summon Courage and climb the highest gate,

Despite the hobbled gait, the awful state,

To be a Woman unfazed by Fate, ungraced by hate:

To know that Fate breeds the faith to be Great.

SONETA 202

For this, my son, were you born: the time

Is long, seasons hard, journey far,—waiting, frustrated,

Like Prince of Egypt, anxious to save his kin,

So struck the Egyptian, before his time, in cold crime;

But soon hated, wisely hasted, till he was maturated,

To lead a people, redeem to glory — new life begin.

SONETA 203

Tell us of the world beyond the moon
Where the stars dance around the lagoon
And swoon at noon, flattered by the breeze
From the trees that kiss the still waters, and tease.
Oh Poeta, speak to us of the dream you've seen,
The land you've been, where joy skips like a teen.

SONETA 204

What kind of Child is this? What manner of Man
Shall be, who lies in manger clothes, and sweetly doze
On Mary's lap? To whom the angels sing, shepherds run —
Glory to God in highest, peace on Earth, to those
He chose! Of whom prophets of old foretold, this Christ,
Our King, our kin, shall save our souls,—be sacrificed.

SONETA 205

O little town of Bethlehem, are you not least

Of your brethren? Your star we've seen in the east,

And come with gifts — for Him born King of Jews —

Whose Israel consist not of blood, but whosoever shall choose

This free Gift of life — peace, goodwill, joy — toward men;

For unto us a child is born,—son is given.

SONETA 206

The fire crackles, the log whistles, the birds chuckle

At news of your coming, which, like Yuletide

Gladdens the weary year with tidings of sweet jingle,

Singing: *Lord Savior is born! Peace to all men betide!*

Thus I, joyous at your coming, like the Second Coming,

Hardly wait, but haste to wake, to see your homecoming.

SONETA 207

I'll be home for Christmas, where bows tied with strings,

Snow high to knees, deck December's trees with shiny things.

I'll be home for Christmas, to hear the children sing,

Santa Claus bring, his plenty gifts, fit for newborn King.

I'll be home for Christmas, my darling queen, at half

Past three, kiss below the mistletoe,—hear Rudolph laugh.

SONETA 208

I find freedom in constraint, boundless joy unbound
Between the walls of sound, within the troughs of rhyme;
Yet I know, with my pen, bright Apollo I confound,
When my writ, tingle the ears of angels; — like mime,
Caress the minds of Muses; much so, dead poets, envious,
Wish were me, and me in their verses were plenteous.

SONETA 209

I saw the face of God today, by chance.

She had on a reddish dress, then was yellow

And green and orange and brown, all at once!

She stood tall beyond the curvy road, in a row,

Waving hello with leafy joy to sweet October air;

I stared, and stared, as she entered November's lair.

SONETA 210

In my winter, I have discovered summer.
In the frightening frost of my discontent
I've seen a forest of bees, a choir of trees,
A patchwork of earth, worker bees — a humming cluster —
Sipping honey, eating pollen's bread. In the descent
To my despair, I felt the balm of bees.

SONETA 211

There's laughter in Rafah. Children are chipper.

Behind the barbed wire fence

That shadows the border, there's clapping,

Singing, dancing; joy in Gaza, without the flower.

Shahad whispers *I do* to Ahmed, in the city of tents,

Surrounded by war, united in love. Hearts are cheering.

SONETA 212

Not bombs and guns, tanks and drones, ships and subs
Shall shave your name from my bones, nor gases
That choke, germs that bleed the lungs like thirsty mobs,
Sully your living diary, or turn your pages to ashes;
For in my heart are you enthroned: impregnable as fortress,
Unconquerable as vastness, unforgettable as goddess.

SONETA 213

Born too early, must be strong to see the morn —
Rise up! Run for cover. Break through this ICU
Laid waste by bombs, to another besieged and torn.
You are Life's band of brothers and sisters, neonatal, too
In a footrace against Death, to beat his chariot horse.
Can't slumber! Must cross this border, or ride his hearse.

SONETA 214

How do kangaroos in love hop on hind feet,

Paw-in-paw, and keep from tipping over, when crossing over?

How do porcupines in heat make love, warm and sweet,

With quills all over, and keep from hurting each other?

How do wolves make war, then make up, howl together,

Like songbirds in chorus, sing in tandem, nuzzle with fervor?

SONETA 215

Were this your homily, Sweet Emily —

Addressed not to you but your Progeny

This fair Child of your gallantry — Your Poetry —

That should proclaim your Memory — your melody —

Though you were reticent — to rather Die with posterity —

Than let bastard pens profane Your Humanity.

SONETA 216

Black queen, gotta holla at you for a minute.
I know you've been walking long in them heels,
You've got dreams — but haters say you'll never make it.
Feet hurt, back aches, skipping meals to pay them bills,
But somehow, you still show up when they say "Quit!"
Girl?? Damn what they say! They don't know your grit.

SONETA 217

My beloved lies to me, yet I cannot tell her

She lies, while she lies … next to me.

For her lie belies her truest power —

Sweet as pumpkin, strong as cider;

So together we lie, with each other,

When she asks me — if I'd ever spied a fairy.

SONETA 218

I thought I saw you look at me

With starry eyes that know my name.

I saw, or thought I saw, cheeks rosy,

Traced out to kiss lips with a pinkish flame.

I thought, for a moment, my thought you could see

Staring at the #BrownEyedGirl in the frame.

SONETA 219

What shall I call you and your name describe?

No, not that name which the world has heard proclaimed —

Though beautiful, still half your claim prescribe;

When you, first of your name that cannot be named,

Are for this world too fine, too kind, to define;

What then shall I call you, sweet love, save mine?

SONETA 220

Not for pomp, not for circumstance,

Not for gilded majesty of crimson-clad carriages

On beaded horses, marching down the street,

To waving bands of adoring fans; still not for chance

Of solemn rite, at ancient Abbey, site of noble marriages,

Do I profess to love you. I love you — stripped.

SONETA 221

Beautiful things that do bloom in May

Bear in their flower nature's fickle grace,

Whose fiat does decree where and when to stay.

But you, sovereign mistress over days,

Do with your power unfurl your very own bud

And so tame the tides of time — with your blood.

SONETA 222

Nature's flower is not without flaw

So why hate you for that which you do show?

As beauty's rose must from bud grow

And at bloom is with thorns, so you, beauty's brilliance,

Are thorned from youth with sweet essence —

Confounding haters by your wit's fragrance.

S O N E T A   2 2 3

Palette for palette, hue for hue, paint for paint,

What color does your beauty lack that I should impart?

Do gods and mortal men before you not faint?

What then shall my forgery add to God's art,

To make foul what Nature herself does envy?

Count them mad, and blind, who counter your regency.

SONETA 224

Let my verse be the glass that reflects

Your truest beaut. In those other glasses

Are a portion of you, what your outward rose projects,

Which does show you grow as the day passes;

But in my verse is your eternal glow shown,

Revealing to you what slothful glass cannot clone.

SONETA 225

From beautiful beings we draw forth joy

So lukewarm hearts may by heaven's earthly envoy

Be heartily warmed. For you, enjoying all grace,

Both in face and in spades, do hold all my gaze

In your solemn worship, wherein day and night,

All day is like night, till I behold your sight.

SONETA 226

In your absent presence a fair debate is born

Between all the parts of me, which in truth,

Though adverse parties, to your dear beauty are sworn;

One argues for your eyes, another for your youth,

Another your cheeks, still another your lips;

Yet do these agree, your picture smiles, while Mona weeps.

SONETA 227

Ages to come will call me a liar

And my rhyme rabid fever of an ailing bard;

Had it been at that time there were a Seer

Who upon my verse shall look with just regard

And through mystic eyes your picture see,

As is, today, and shall so swear your ageless beauty.

SONETA 228

Those pictures that store your memory

Recite only but a stanza of your melody;

And though with telepathy tell of your beauty,

They are hollow rooms echoing your symphony,

Playing a single movement of your sweet harmony.

Ah! They're deaf, and blind, who haven't shared your company.

SONETA 229

I may never learn to play the piano's white keys
And so with fine notes croon of your sweetness;
Nor the black keys of the organ play with ease
To swoon your heart with a lover's smoothness;
But this much I know how to do:
Write with black pen, on white paper, *I love you*.

SONETA 230

Some poets with their praises bring a tomb

For fear their fragile flower her fair would lose,

And thus, with their rhymes, enshrine their helpless muse.

But such grace had you from womb,

My dullest line your peerless name gives breath.

Let others their muses mourn; in my lines, defy death.

SONETA 231

There's a madness you yourself conjure, dear queen,

Which no pharmacy, or physician, can mend;

The stars of heaven glow not like your Calabar skin,

Nor Aphrodite with your fair wonder contend;

With what Ancient Wonder shall I then compare you,

But in wondering admit — all praises — your praise outdo.

SONETA 232

I swear we must be one, though our names differ;

For within your lines flows the rhythm of the Nile,

Swelling so with richness and style;

But I, barren and void of truth and star,

Do from your sweet self some sweetness steal,

To give my verse a flair fit for your highness still.

SONETA 233

As you are new, so is my rhyme,

Which does not count long English lines

Or to freshness add stiff meter from antique time;

But as darling buds of May do burst the vines

With fresh grapes, fit for new wine, so you,

Sweetly new like dew, bless my song anew.

SONETA 234

How I've often looked at you
Through eyes too deep to see.
The very sight of you besieges me,
Then, myself, by myself, what can I do?
But with the whole wide world agree —
Picassos are ugly standing next to you.

SONETA 235

I must admit and cannot lie,

My verse against my rhyme do war:

My verse, attired in royal dye,

Says it does speak of you the more,

My rhyme, your sweetness tell the best —

Thus twain, though in contest, your fame duly attest.

SONETA 236

When to those hallowed pipes I listen
Which tingle the sacred hollows of the cathedral,
And mass choirs hear sing with harmony
The joyful news of Jesus Christ arisen;
Then your sweet soft mellow voice do I hear withal,
Which sounds so as angels at symphony.

SONETA 237

Sleep is for those who are weary of you

(Those destined to forever feast upon your look);

For your beauty can no eye ceaselessly view

Or your speeches' brilliance boldly brook;

Permit then these weary eyes to sleep escape

Where dreams of you are as heaven's landscape.

SONETA 238

From your mind I shall not be undone

Though spheres of you do plot with fate

To blot my name, my memory, from your brain

While yet our playful hearts do waltz, as one —

Star-struck lovers stalled at heaven's gate;

Then am I not afraid, assured, in you shall remain.

SONETA 239

It is true that you are loud when you would

Rather be quiet. To the world silent, undetected,

Like air, fill the year with unspoken dream;

Alas, your beauty betrays you like fire betrays wood,

Blaring your presence wherever you are sighted —

This your poet knows, yet, joins the world to scheme.

SONETA 240

Queen of my days, to whom shall I sing
Of your praise, and your face appraise
Like any other gaze, or to your court bring
Beggarly praise of kings gone mad, and queens malaise?
For by your light, we shall see, by your power,
We shall breathe. Bless this day with your dateless flower.

SONETA 241

I've had my way with you with words

Stroking your inmost chord with love;

Listening, ear pressed against your chest,

Waiting, for that rhythm your heart records.

And, like a maestro, blessed with sense from above,

Sweet music make from the flutter of your breast.

S O N E T A   2 4 2

Every time I sit to write of you

I find most vile, rude, and crude

This barren pen that does exude

The wretched print of a mourner's hue.

Were my pen the shades of the rainbow

In my sweet poem your eternal glow would show.

SONETA 243

To write of you and feel the world

Ignore my writ, when you're the force within the word

That all mouths speak and all eyes read —

From Babel to babble, in speech and in-deed;

Are you not twice the fable of ancient lore?

A city on a hill that cannot be hid — forevermore?

SONETA 244

It cannot be said you glow as the sun

When you summer better than the hottest weather;

How can it be that you comfort like a nun

When you succor better than the highest prayer?

Oh let it be said my love is as one,

Of one, and of everyone, is as none.

SONETA 245

I have come to your house with my calabash
In hand. I have brought some meals: pounded yam
With egusi soup; jollof rice with curried fish,
Bush meat, some palm wine. I see the table of lamb,
Creamy salad, truffle biscuits, with 2010 Chardonnay.
I'm hungry, my friend! Let's eat. First, we must pray.

SONETA 246

Oríṣà bí ìyá kò máa sí láàyé

All worldly splendors, to your myriad wonders, defer.

In your sunlight, the brightness of their powers cower;

In your aura, Mama, all fortunes surrender.

Now, in your flora, are beauty's petals arrayed,

Like sparkling diamonds upon a coral reef. Yèyé ní wúrà!

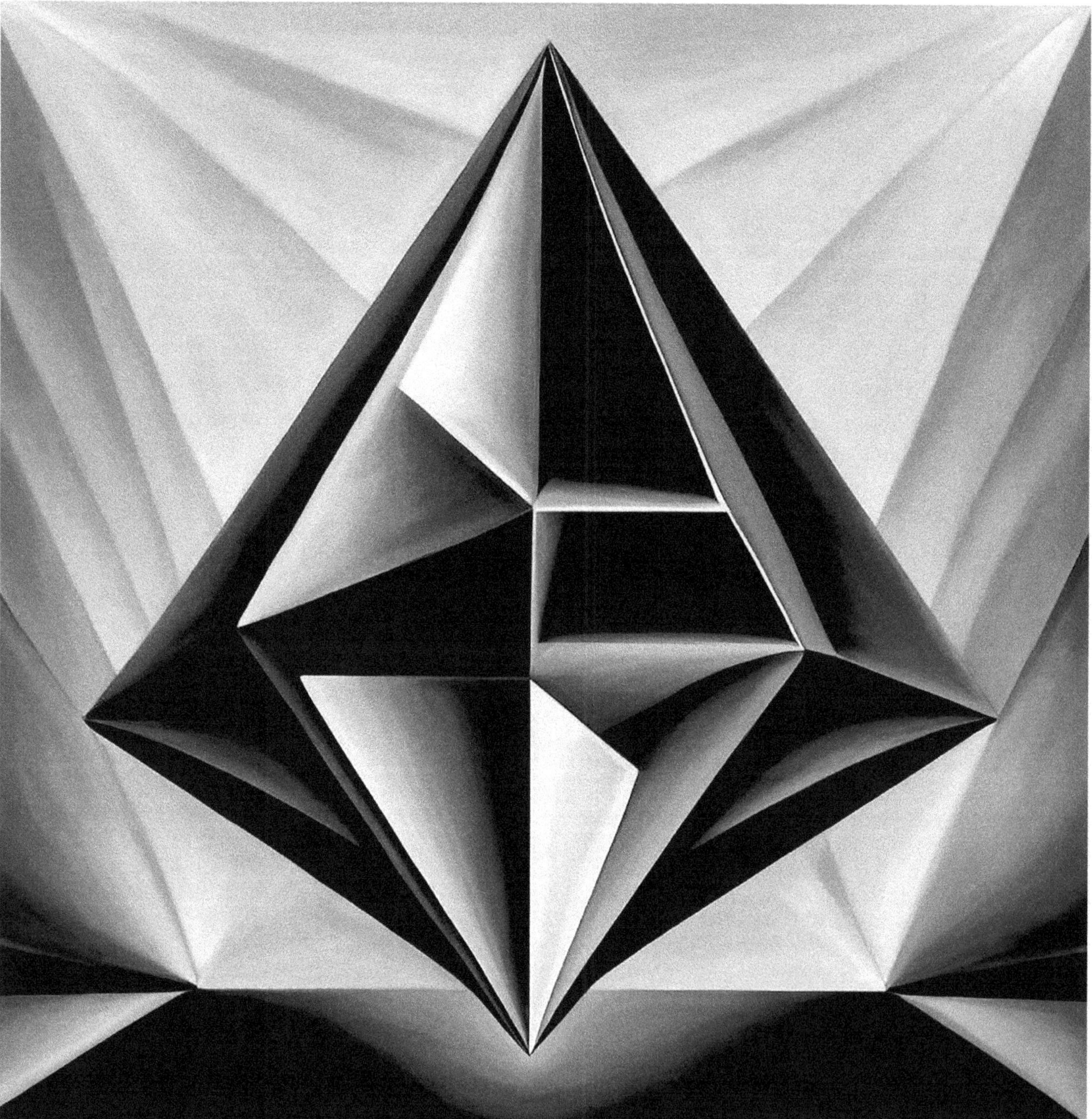

MOVEMENT VI:

Prisma

DAWN OF LOVE

ALTHOUGH soothing night to my eyes beckon,

Yet to her cries cruelly lend not a weary eye—

My hands, worn with day, with night duly reckon;

Thus twain plead for their master's bed to lie.

Nevertheless do I toil, pushing slothful Dawn along—

My eyes with my hands do I brashly brush,

Hurrying ignorant Dawn to the sweets of her tongue,

The velvety embrace of bosom so plush,

The gaze in her eyes that to these eyes

New life give; and on her fair do hungrily feed.

O Dawn! If thou know'st what ahead of thee lies,

Thy sloth wilt abandon and make great speed.

    Love, love—what morn begins not with thee,

    When the larks of heaven await thy decree.

EYES OF LOVE

MY love's brows are as dark night,

Yet have I seen no starry sight

Nor sparkle beheld with such bright,

As that which my love's eyes ignite;

Precious diamond hath great might

Yet are my love's eyes unequaled in delight;

Her eyes sprightly bright give light,

And heaven's eye thus slight in height;

Who writes to posterity and of her eyes not write—

So ages ageless rime should recite?

Or what poet sacred beauty dare incite,

And to my love's eyes not do due rite?

  All my loves are my love's right;

  Her eyes mine eyes daily excite.

EYES OF THE HEART

BUT that my heart once loved, it lied

And partook of my eyes' foolishness,

Sending gullible tongue on wasteful stride,

So base lies to the world should profess;

For then, my heart, unsighted to simple truth,

On the judgement of my eyes did rely,

And my eyes, flattered by such worth,

Painted true where falsehood did lie.

But now is my heart made my eyes,

And true visions truly made new—

Where before old loves were lies

You, my love, are love's proven view.

   This confession now has my tongue:

   You alone are my heart's song.

HEAVEN'S CARESS

HAD my love's show been wrought of clay,

Moulded from its brightest and most precious metal;

Gold, silver, diamond,—all, or more than this array:

Then her worth, if of any be,—be but little.

For these worthless-precious, shiniest in men's hearts

(Mined from mire and having with worms dined),

Are by eyes glorified for all their earthly parts;

Much so, evil to their shine be inclined.

But no! Such flaws hath not my love's show,

For heaven in her making had for eyes made

Two faultless stars that should forever glow,

And her skin bore from the silkiest cloud:

    So when my lips on my love's lips I place,

      Nothing of this world I kiss, but heaven's face.

THE LORD'S MASTERPIECE

IF every Muse were as temperate as thee

Where then do they hide their pride?

Thy poet swears so,—many a red be,

But none as that in which thou art dyed:

Thy glow shy red give day's bright.

And when thou speakest thy speech so,

And thy lips watch go, summer's might

With thy soft winds dost thou gently blow.

What June may then with thee compete, my Muse,

If all her beauty to thy beauty owed debt,

And all her roses, though as soothing prose,

To thy red no match hath met?

  O fair that doth hold beauty outweighed—

  In thine eyes is something the Lord made.

IMMACULATE BEAUTY

THAT thou art too beautiful to behold
Shall not be thine undoing fault.
Look, heaven's eye doth boldly boast its gold
And bare eyes dare not scold it for such gloat;
See'st not as all eyes seek its warmth
And cherish the glitter from its saunter above?
What eyes beckon the frost from winter's froth
And wicked night over kind day would rather love?
Be true! Even as thou art all of sacred Truth,
And watch all of false Art wither in thy glow;
But smite not thy poet with thy youth—
Save me, for thee, so thy praise may still grow.
  In others' lines art thou aided with new trend;
  To age thee so, when thy beauty needs no mend.

OMNIPRESENT BEAUTY

WHO are you? What are you made of,

That every beautiful thing of God should your semblance bear,

Speaking sweet words of you with sweet love,

You in everything, everything … in you,—everywhere?

Feel heaven open up its dam in febrile July,

And therein you are, blessing man and vine alike;

Hear the laughter of playful children pierce the evening sky,

And, even so, do babes after your innocence take;

In every fair face do you have a part,

As every fair is but a preview of your fair,

Forewarning this world of such flawless art

Which only in you is found, in colour so rare.

   Lo, even here you are, in this pleasant rime,

   Fortifying my rime against destructive time.

DEFIANT BEAUTY

WHEN I raise mine eyes to survey beauty's bounteous field,
And summer's flower behold all pompous in prime,
And every favoured thing with sweet flavour revealed—
Wherein my Muse's face doth shine sublime;
When thinking on things to come, things that were,
Methinks Picasso had not a stroke
As curvy as her chin,—nor Raphael a ware
With such a colour as lives within my Muse's cheek;
When joying in this, myself pride most prideful of men,
Deeming her sweeter than what praise can tell
Or sweet tongue confess,—even as this proof pen,
In lines that shall outbrave the fiery darts of hell;
    Then, wary of Time's injurious hand, I go straight sad:
    Fearing to Nature's best art, Time his blot will add.

E N V Y   O F   T H E   M U S E S

SO many times have I invoked you for my Muse,
So many times my pen have you possessed,
And that foul which black ink doth produce,
Under your fair spell hath been fairly blessed;
Then, 'tis no wonder that I of myself cannot write,
When my barren self can but barrenness to myself lend
Clouding with rude ignorance what is already bright—
Wherefore profane that which your gentle spirit doth attend?
For all my verses are but one dear argument,
Tending that which your rich self doth infuse,
Proving you ten times the nine muses other rimers present,
When for habitation my lines did choose.
    Such conceit have I of that which I compile
    Borne of you; methinks dead poets envy my style.

ETERNAL LIFE

WORRY not, my love! This masterful rime of mine
Shall thy living record be, when jealous Death
Thy sweet frame shall deem too fine
And tombs of brass shall battle for thy breath.
In these lines shalt thou shine more bright
Than a thousand ages of the antique sun
And feel thy blood warm still, in spite
Of these bastard signs that shall claim thou art done.
Be content in these contents, ensconced in the knowledge
That a greater force doth use my pen,
And with it doth make thee a sacred pledge:
Thou shalt forever live in the hearts of men.
  If this be blasphemy,—so be it!
  Mine own life shall underwrite my writ.

TRANSIENT SPLENDOUR

THEN upon thy face do I gaze

And of thy beauty question make

When July's green upon which the herd did graze,

November's cold now gathers with rake;

And I behold the falling star that so glittered,

Unto lowly earth fall and lie in tatters;

And see mighty rivers which erst nurtured

The fields with water, asleep in their sepulchres;

And feathered choirs see flee naked trees

Where luscious leaves once kissed the flirty wind;

Then anew do I question make of thy short lease,

Which thou treasurest so, but to thee be unkind.

   From Time's kiss can thy lips make no shield

    When all good things to his charm do yield.

MORTAL FOLLY

FOOLISH soul, sojourner within these carnal walls,

Beguiled by these rebel forces that do hold thee bound—

Why dost thou surfeit on matters so false,

And fill thy fleeting store with substance so compound?

Look around thee, beyond these mortal walls and these rebels;

See as darling lilies fester like base weeds,

Demoted from old glory to worthless rubble,

And tyrants' busts toppled from atop their vaunted steeds.

See strong men of strong will

Give way to impotence and fear in old age:

Alack, why then like steel treat'st thou thy flower still,

When Death thy wealth shall not deem his due wage?

  Clueless soul, why slave thee to build mansions

  Whilst another starves of urgent rations?

DISGRACEFUL DAY

O DISGRACEFUL Day! How faithless art thou!

Why with brightness so lovely and temperate

And winds so cooling and restful didst thou wow,

But in thine heart allowed stay for hate?

Why didst coward Death let wander in thy cool,

And his theft plot away from wary eyes,

And watched innocent youth lured to the pool,

Where from Death's grip never did rise?

Alas, how do I wish thy sin away,

When within thee lies the heart of Brutus?

Thy face, which doth kindly shine today,

Once upon a time did hide Death's rotten pus.

   O brother! Of brothers have I no other but thee:

   Thine absence weep still when thy face in sleep I see.

SORROW'S ALCHEMY

THUS shall I, bludgeoned by the gangs of fate,

Know how hard true sorrow hits

When every word that doth proceed, screams hate!

And pampered tongue shuns sweetest sweets.

Eyes that reckoned beauty doth live in faultless art

Now with fortune join to say,

'O no! A thousand times more beauty assert,

The darkness that lightens a hideous day.'

And so is sorrow shown stronger

Than mighty wars that bow the heads of kings,

Or mountains of brass welded together—

When sorrow falls not as drops, but showering throngs.

  Dear friend, that thou lov'st still is misplaced,

  Where ancient friends flee in frenzied haste.

CAPTIVE HEART'S REBELLION

NO longer will I look at you,

Lest my mind be further corrupted.

Not that your youthful fair hath lost its hue,

For all tongues still give you your sole due.

In my thoughts will I not be tempted

To again pattern my walk with your walk,

And sluggish Chance lend a hand unwanted,

To force your looks upon eyes dejected.

Thus, my loving thoughts, trapped in your lock,

Shall I set free and give leave to wander,

As a sprout does from the grasp of earth break,

And his boughs unfold, so in the sun may bask.

  O Pity me! Such madness, that today your adversary rave,

  Tomorrow, your eager captive crave.

DESIRE'S DILEMMA

IS it for this my dear time is spent,
To be a strait through which all ships do pass?
With what is mine do I find least content,
Coveting without end every God's gracious lass.
Lush maidens mine eyes daily tempt,
Forever desiring every fair on which they lay,
And mine eyes do hold mine heart in contempt,
When on lust's luscious field let not hay.
Surely, there was a time I knew true peace,
And from life's muggy fog did break through
To clear one shining path to see God's face—
Lo! Must I now bid that time adieu?
  Nothing gives, and of self not given,
  Save from another borrow to stay even.

INDOMITABLE ESSENCE

THEN will this imperfect world, as flawed as she is,

Mine imperfections demand I make perfect,

So her straight teeth my crooked teeth may kiss

And her light skin my dark skin respect.

When upon my name doth she look, and frown—

'Hast thou not a prettier name may pronounce?'

And at my tongue laugh, like the thoughtless clown,

'Thy speech echoes not like the English Crowns!'

Thus shall the world and I forever at war stay:

She, my being, unwilling to take as is, and I,

Unwilling mine essence to sell for peace,—fray;

Till that time shall come, when tearing from eye to eye,

    Mourners shall say: Here lies a man without peer,

    Here lives the man the world could not steer.

AFRICA'S LAMENT

DEAR God! Why hast thou forsaken the origin of man,

And thy tent removed from the clouds above the land?

Across thy creation dark gloom doth span,

And evil dines at ease with the hearts of mankind.

Didst thou leave with the last of the Pharaohs?

Watched from afar, as 'Stanley Meets Mutesa,'

Bearing the bulky chests of sorrows,

To be bartered for the soul of the Savanna?

I, a son of the land, darkened by the stare

Of the smoldering sun, helplessly call on Thee,

For war, greed, and pestilence do choke the evening air,

And crude and uncouth do neighbours call me.

    Forsake not the works of thine hands, O Lord!

    Lest Africa in her pain forever lie unheard.

AFRICA SAMBA

AH! From the distant lands I hear the rumble,

The batter of the samba as she passes these leaves,

Her voice these roots cause to tremble:

Lo! Such that chases a thousand thieves.

I see the young lion out of his den come forth

The springhare from his hole in the ground peer,

The giraffe with grace stride from the north;

And from atop this luscious perch drew me near.

Together our feet joined this hallowed ground,

Soaked in the sweet sounds of the samba,

Our limbs danced and curled to a magic unbound,

As when the African sun basks the mamba.

    O Africa! How dare I love thee in quiet words:

    Of thy praises in kingly rimes, there are no lords!

RAINBOWS AND SHADOWS

METHINKS my life is a crowded canvas

Stroked with diverse colours of different hues,

Strewn on by errant brushes that do pass;

Each, my joy, my pain, freely use as muse.

With Hell's black do some paint at will,

Whilst others lighten with night's dark;

And then, with Heaven's rainbow do some fill,

So upon view, thou see'st me sitting on God's arc.

Yet, of this art may not swiftly dispose,

Though its warring shades its frame make weak

And from its smoothness make known all woes—

Still, at world's end, of its use must speak.

   Then, dear friend, let this happy occasion be:

   My life was well spent with thee.

LOVE'S DIVINE ACCORD

WHEN I say I love you, pretty one,

Know not in God's very ears I swear?

What mortal man may seek undone

That which by Heaven's just creed bear?

To love you is to be at peace with God,

A treaty betwixt Him and me,

As betwixt the soil on which must bud

The apple tree, so its roots may be.

For what man such war brings,

The full wrath of Heaven's host

On flesh made of flimsy strings,

And bones no warrior dare boast?

   In loving you, sweet love, I love Him;

   And in loving Him, I sing heaven's hymn.

IMMUTABLE LOVE

TYRANT Time! Go on, do thy worst!
What more canst thou take, what vein
Canst thou bleed to please thy mortal thirst—
Whose depth with death doth not wane?
Do princes not thy grace court with precious gold,
And troubadours thine ears croon with dreamy ballads?
Still, kingdoms dost thou devour with injurious mould
And voices like angels' dull into hollow sounds.
Yet, hear this, remorseless Time: My love
Canst thou not smear with the decay of empty days,
Nor canst thou thy decree upon her prove,
Whilst thou and thy minions on all others graze:
  For in this verse is my love made immortal
  Where maggots of this world do not crawl.

IN EVERY ELEMENT, YOU

WHAT hears and to thy voice not dance?

Or flows and into thine ocean not go?

Or talks and thy praises not proudly advance?

Or breathes and from thine air not borrow?

Or sees and heaven's sight not behold in thy view?

Or runs and into thy sunshine not rush?

Or feels and the warmth of thy lips bid adieu?

Or sleeps and against thy face in dream not brush?

Sweet love, against myself thy defence so take,

Chiding my befuddled self beforehand

Lest in some ignorant hour, thy truth forsake,

And against thee offences rudely demand:

    For I think on thee as the monk his text,

    Finding joy where cannot be vexed.

SAILING TO LOVE'S SHORE

WHEN I board that ship that sails for my youth

And this present land of means leave,

Over wailing oceans and frightful seas doth

My spirit travel, to places once did live;

Onto continents and into cities do I roam,

Where maidens fair and plumb,

Tall and short, beautiful as the art of Rome,

Gather, but together are none of thy sum.

O am I happiest! When to thy door

It brings me, and to thy soft lips I give soft words,

And to thy sweet face I hold all else sour:

Forgetting cares of all treacherous worlds.

   Then, as doth become the sailor starved of sand,

   So doth it me, when thy shore needs leave behind.

ECHOES OF ADIEU

IF you've missed me as I have you,

Then you must have passed a hell of a time!

And like a mammal in winter, anxious for the prime,

Counted those countless hours since we both said adieu.

For from you have I been farthest in April

While yet the blushful rose did bloom,

And the buds of the lilac, flattered in whitish costume,

Did charge the vernal air with a fragrant zeal.

But now is it August, when summer's golden sky

Do boldly remind me of your glow

And laughter of birds hugging the hedge below,

Do echo what joy was here before you said goodbye.

   Winter cometh. But what winter I fear,

   When the while without you was winter here.

WHEN THE STRAY BIRD SINGS

IN the event of my demise,

Perchance, while abroad, some stray bird

Should your ears solemnly advise

That from this strange world I am fled—

Where evil doth reign as day

And good cowers as frightful night;

To my buried wrongs give no say,

Lest in your thoughts I be forgotten quite.

But think of me as such:

That I did from all foolishness retreat

And sought to prove much

What spice hath that life—with you in it.

  And this I wish the world know—

  For I loved you so.

FLEETING CHARMS

HOW like the fleeting season art thou,

That today thy show not show,

That that,—by which thou dost wow

To thy cruel self bury so.

Were thine hips not for this carved,

Then would I not say so, that my groin,

Cold and with the barren day starved,

May with the warmth of thine hips join,

And my lips to thy lips speak

And mine outward thine inmost meet,

So love's healing potion, made potent at love's peak,

May bare bones by its fullness replete.

    But thou brute, in love with thine own worth,

    Wouldest the world writhe in thy dearth.

FORTY WINTERS OF THE HEART

HOW like forty winters hath thine absence felt!
What bitter December's flakes have I tasted!
What blows hath frigid frost my fragile frame dealt!
Yet was this summer's time, and thou art departed.
The crimson birds that did sing, and beat heaven's drum,
With feathered hands, no longer sweet music make:
From thy speech, lyrics did brew; alas, thou art dumb!
With thine heart away, no drum or beat so quake.
Heaven's eye it seems, doth slowly break his stare,
Seeing thy shadow he sees not below.
So are days darker with day, bringing winter much near,
When all of summer's splendours await thy show.
  What darkness compass me with thee gone,
  Darker than the blackest 'clipse that stains the sun!

SIGHS AND CONSOLATIONS

WHEN I sigh in frustration and my troubles lament

And through others' joy and laughter

My own gripping hollow of sadness feel torment,

And at heaven's blind eyes heave darts in anger,

Then do I weep as a spring for cousins not seen,

Doting aunts, chivalrous uncles, tucked away

In Fate's hateful vise—as the mean lord holds a lien,

My kin keep as though his debt I yet to pay.

Then through night's rotten dark, dream faces of places,

Adorned with endless oceans and bluest seas,

Hills and mountains with happy trees and witty daises

And cause anew, to curse beauties that cruelly tease.

  What sight do I see and cease to moan?

  My love's show—all grief doth hastily dethrone.

MUTUAL FUTURES

LET those whom Nature hath wittingly deemed fit
To husband her expanse, glory in their uncommon birth;
Whom Fortune with her uneven hands hath made elite,
Flatter their fragile hearts with boisterous mirth;
But thou, dearest friend, I pray thee, do not so!
Rather, number thy numbered days with numbers divine;
Prove thy worth more than dregs can show,
Which, after all, can this earthly earth to thee consign.
Look in another eye and therein thy reflection see,
Painting thee in another hue, calling thee to thyself;
That thou, by blessing another, bless'st thine own body,
And, gainer be, when thou shalt someday seek relief.
  For as Life is individual, so is she dual:
  Wherein our future is perforce mutual.

INDEPENDENT MUSE

MY Muse swears she is independent—

And so wears her worth like a newfound watch;

Flaunting that to which all her care is bent:

'I can this,' 'I can that,'—doth she staunchly vouch.

Alack! What sweet poverty hath my Muse's tongue,

That her most beautiful flower should fairest grow,

Tyrant to herself, removed from whence she doth belong,

From that which doth nurture, and her graces well show.

The wild rose her nectar may deem sweetest,

Yet, from her riches can no honey gather,

Save the honeybee on her tender bosom rest,

And her sweetest sweet make even sweeter.

   Sad it be, if for thee I borrow heaven's air,

   And yet, thou say'st thou need'st no care.

OLATINPO'S DILEMMA

WHY as the Bard do I write

And my style few departures take?

In my lines, his, doth shine bright,

And his restful soul I so awake;

When to these old thoughts—

Once writ in old Queen's words—

Stubborn me selfishly lend new plots,

As though in cabal with Time's birds

To fetch him thence,

And into this sorrowful world place.

Alas! What laws summon in defence,

That renders refuge, or tenders grace?

  Dear Bard, mine appeal doth submit,

  These poor rude lines only seek half thy wit.

COUNTERFEIT BEAUTY

LIKE water for life

Food for health

So were you to my every breath:

A chameleon for wife.

Has Beauty not one face,

Wherein God's work is shown

And His perfect love made freely known—

A vision of heaven's gentle grace?

How then, dear friend, are you two-faced—

By your rank deeds bring such shame;

Giving Beauty a bastard name—

That in you Beauty should be so disgraced?

   Beauty wishes well,

    Yet do men look at you—and see hell.

DAWN'S EMBRACE

WHEN thou shalt rise in the early morn—
And from thy brief leave to heaven's lair
Art made swiftly returned by love's lonesome mourn,
Which this heart thine absence doth loudly blare;
Then for such rudeness canst thou not grieve—
For righteous day wrongful night doth daily forgive,
Even as murky night, bright day doth nightly aggrieve;
Lo! On the morrow, his shine doth newly give.
For thou, being too sweet, hast my buds pampered;
And when in peaceful sleep thine eyes do sleep,
Then do I feel most sorrowed, and bothered,
That sweet sleep, being favoured, my love doth keep.
  Ah! Thou awakened, no longer such matter:
  Asleep, a distant lover; awake, a doting lover.

SORROW'S SUMMER SOLSTICE

GIVE me the blustery warmth of a winter day,

Therein may find summer's comfort.

The winter night to the cheerful bee lends no play—

Though it be cold, yet in the day's sun cavort.

Thus my sorrow into these wretched lines etch

As this night of colds coldest, and darks darkest,

Robs me of day's happier snow, and into a wretch

Turn, when teary eyes lend not a sunny rest.

Icy Death and winter night to me are one:

The latter, as the guillotine holds the offender in place,

So from the knife's blade he may not run—

So doth she brace me for the former's cold embrace.

    Sweet thoughts of thee think, —like spring,

    Winter's woes fade, and into thy summer spring.

AUTUMN'S ELEGY

THAT window in time thou mayest in me see,

When greedy clouds to piteous earth no showers lend,

And those green things that on the boughs did be,

Yellow now made by nature's arid end.

In me thou see'st the flicker of such light

Once the glow that owned the dark

Now sullen slave to night's bright,

No longer Master of sparkling spark.

In me thou see'st the bare of that beach,

Once a paradise on which two adoring lovers lay,

Her glistening sands bathed in sweet peach,

Carried away hence by ocean's callous sleigh.

  This thou knowest well, like worn stories of old,

   Yet, with mine aches, is thy love newly told.

OF EARTHLY PRAISES AND HIDDEN FLAWS

THEN of what earthly dues are their breaths,
To whom are the loftiest heights of mountains;
Names may only don with beauteous wreaths,
And to Time's taunts feel no pains?
They are Heaven's magistrates to life,
Rightly going, and coming, as they please.
Judging others but to themselves no strife
Impute. Of their countenance others lease,
But from their grips never seize lordship.
The groomed dog is to the mistress cute
Though her image only would it worship,
But if rabid, the smelliest skunk its bark mute:
　　For cutest things by their acts become ugliest,
　　Chihuahuas that kill make skunks far dearest.

REDEMPTIVE NOVEMBER

GRIMMEST things may in season redeem

And from old stench spring forth new fragrance;

So that which in time past, foul we did deem,

Sweet scent now give, and on new grace chance.

Alas, Fourth! April's truth thou didst smother,

Smiting sweet peace with thy piece—

Thy coward filth into brave King did wander,

So scornful death could love's crown seize.

Lo! Wast thou not to July's cry born,

With Liberty's joyous song in thy lungs?

Yet, to that Creed which thou wast sworn,

Its true meaning hast made lies by thy wrongs.

   Ah! But that gift which to November didst give,

   Redolent it is, and all wrongs maketh to forgive.

VERDICT AND MERCY

ACCUSE me thus: that I, a vagabond,

The estate of your love did squander,

Spending unthriftily the sum of your bond

Which largess upon absent-minded me did confer.

That I have given to women of lesser birth,

Lesser warmth for eyes, lesser grace of ease,

The treasure of noble truth, of sacred worth

Which to you, for you, your leisure should please.

Charge me as doth befit a conquered tyrant;

Witness call the reckless deeds of younger days

So my weight on stark tree should mount,

And the world your verdict join to set me ablaze.

  But wait! Mine advocate in you for me pleads:

  Saying—tender mercy doth bleed for my deeds.

UNGRATEFUL LOVE

UNGRATEFUL love, dare say ye I love thee not,
When wherever I be, though there I am present,
Still from there am I absent, when my thought,
Always with thee, shuns new subject to invent?
Then of myself take I no thought, nor the injury
That I do myself count injury for love's sacred joy;
Seeing as no heed I take of that sweet melody,
Which my appetence doth sing; nor the lowliest pleasures enjoy.
But thou alone in this world art all my care,
And till I'm returned to thee, what pleasure I know,
What comfort I feel, save when with thee new share
Those precious moments Time doth steal whenever I go.
  My love is as a slave—dutiful to thy will—
  Yet, thou prov'st a mistress harder than steel.

FORGIVING FAULTS

TO what may I fault mine affection for you,

Sweetest love? Shall I the Crown of Heaven

Blindly charge, lest as the ingrate, I too,

Speak like him who eats of Heaven's daily leaven,

Yet batters Heaven's ears for its sweetness?

Ah! Shall your father be blamed, and then your mother,

For conspiring with nature, to bear such likeness,

Whose fairness wills of steel doth smother?

Or better still, shall dear Fate hold in contempt,

For plotting mine arid path, graced with void,

To chance upon looks even angels may not preempt,

And a heart such joy bringeth, maketh overjoyed?

   To loving you are a million faults,

   All of which I happily forgive for your love's lots.

LOVE'S ETERNAL HUM

AGAINST that time do I guard, when this paper,

Wrought of lowly pulp, shall to yellow turn

And to sullen earth return, to forever

Be with that whence it did spawn.

Against that time—sweet love—do I write,

When all eyes shall darkness claim

As silent night gently grabs hold of day's light

And my love for you can no man any more proclaim.

Against that time my love hide in your heart,

So when this world to doom has come,

And all memories from here made depart—

From the dust of your heart, my love will still hum.

  Kings and princes Time may make slaves,

    My love for you can he seal in no graves.

THE POET'S EPITAPH

WHAT newfound tongue do I employ
Or shameful lines inscribe into my rime
That thine ears I ought afraid may cloy
With a poet's flattery past prime?
Or thine eyes astound—with hideous ink,
In whose blackness all colours are devoured?
Finer than aged wine in a cask,
Knowest thou thy truest worth: thyself thy reward!
Rebuke my rime and thy trespass may not judge:
For all of diction, laden with ages' invention,
To thy pearly eyes is but a dreary smudge;
To thine hallowed ears a speechless mime.
    If lies on thee so heap, mine epitaph so scream:
    'This man never writ. Ten times damn him!'

RICHER THAN RICHES

I HAVE known penury, the clatter of nothingness,
Shaken uneven hands of Desire and hopeless yens,
Stared at dinners of nought and breakfasts of emptiness,
And felt the many pleasures of beggary's thorns.
Every beast I see greets me with seemly sympathy,
Lowering its head and bidding me good with tail,
Sensing in me the rotten scent of piteous tragedy—
The spite of Fortune's woes made loud with wail.
So doth it seem, as was said of old,
Nothing makes defence—against a callous world—save that
Which binds the hearts of men in glittery gold,
And enslaves eyes to its blinding light.
   O, unconquerable love! Show thyself richer than riches,
   Mightier than his sword and flowery speeches!

DEFIANCE

BETTER days have I seen

Better nights have I beheld

Bearing the wondrous gifts of April's green;

The joyous stars that so glittered upon August's head.

Alas, 'tis now the winter of woes,

That throws the souls of men into throe

And buries all of summer's glorious glows

In wretched December's snow.

Still have I seen brave day wrest himself

From the gallows of ghastly night;

And the desert plant with pride look upon herself

Having fought the worst of Nature's spite.

   I do therefore defy thee vagrant Time—

   I shall be unremoved, though you do your gravest crime.

COFFERS OF MY HEART

COUNT it counterfeit that pen that did pen

Those verbose lines of old, boasting in its penmanship

That all my worldly all to you tendered then;

My everything to you rendered in worship.

And as such, within the coffers of my heart,

Emptiness should now share space with nothingness.

Alack! Sweet love. Why! When such wealth doth impart

The rising sun that ushers in with brightness

The burdened day teeming with increase,

Blessing the withered flower with precious shower,

The shaved beard with newer length for lease,

And thus, teaching all pens to henceforth aver:

    By day my all on my love is spent;

    My all, for my love, day doth reinvent.

ODE TO THE YORUBA QUEEN

WHO is he that's so blessed with vision

And fortuned to look upon thy shadow

Immediately offers not to thee oblation

Upon those two fires that burn beneath the brow?

For even the blind speak of thy breed:

The warmth from thy rich form

Pressed upon sightless eyes to feed,

Happies the soul within, and of true beauty doth inform.

Sweet Yoruba queen, no longer shall rimers to come

Employ Helen of Troy, nor her ancient face adore:

Thy face and thy form, combined, double her sum,

And double her ships shall these bring thy shore.

    Ọmọge, slay me with rapturous charm;

    Let me die a thousand deaths in thy loving arm.

EBONY'S ENCHANTMENT

SWEET dark ebon, if before now

Beauty had no name, and no tongue could tell,

Nor great men unto great wisdom avow

What beauty's true hue may so call;

Behold, now shall none seek any further,

Or into question make, or in quandary stay—

For beauty hath robbed as the burglar:

Thy precious name hath she stolen away!

That which was thine, now to beauty doth belong—

Through thine eyes, thievish beauty doth look;

So when all hearts shall for beauty long

Thy face shall see, and thy great name shall speak.

What beauty hath life and with Black not begin?

What was lost, thou givest home again.

LOVE'S LOSS IS LOVE

LOVE, Love—how else may Love be Love

If to your cause it has not lost itself?

If to the lonely sun that saunters above,

It has not stood on the highest shelf

And its core bore, so your joy may feel?

If to windy winter woes, its naked chest

Is yet to set free, but thinketh not to seal,

So it may shiver at your warmth's cold arrest?

For so long have I heard it told,

'Love hurts not.' But is not in this

Love's triumph be known; that it doth hold

Joy and pain,—in one blissful kiss?

    If Love thus mock and so err,

     Hearts be stones and no name I bear.

HYMNS OF YOU

HAVE you heard how I love you?
The birds say before they wake, am I awake
Singing true hymns of you with the morning dew—
Calling on all to sing your praise till daybreak.
Ah, my love! Hear the rivers mumble about my love,
They grumble when I do amble by:
They say,—because 'tis you I think of
No river flows like that which flows within my thigh.
And yes, I've heard the sun whisper to the moon,
Heard him complain mine eyes respect him not,
For mine eyes think the day lukewarm at noon—
Till I see you, and your face makes everything hot!
  For the love of you my life will give;
  For the love of you my all would leave.

BLUEST BLUE

WHY may I not boast, confident in Your love,

Secured as bluest blue on buoyant sea,

Whose hue with the seasons doth not move,

Battered, yet, unbothered doth be,

When chariots of day, of night, with fury do charge—

Bearing that churl, Death himself—

And thumping tempests and thunders discharge

So deep blue from deep sea should wear off?

But greater love hath no man than this:

That a Man lay down His life for His friend

And from the stormy grips of Death release,

So abundant life should by love know no end.

    At Calvary was love made known,

    Assuring this: I never walk alone.

DIVINE BEAUTY

FLAWLESS love, change not thy form, thy way,
Thy being, so thy poor poet may please.
Temporal eyes temporal beauty do betray,
But of thy divine beauty can no eyes decrease.
As thou art, do I love thee, sweet love:
Thy sight and thy smell, thy touch and thy taste,
The bells of thy voice as on a Christmas Eve,
My poesy—like a skinny maid—gives waist.
To what purpose may the darling buds of May
Their flush change, or their new scent alter,
When to frigid November frost they
Give no remembrance, or let loiter?
  If of thy praises thy poet sees to write,
  What wrong dost thou then seek to right?

ODE TO THE ETERNAL SUMMER

WHO shall pair thee with a summer's day,
Art thou not fairer and of greater joy?
Too often do heaven's cheeks turn gray,
And his smoldering eye sometimes annoy.
The summer rose to the summer doth live,
Though it be as beautiful as Jacob's coat;
And sometimes a night's rest deprive,
Choirs atop the cedars that chirp a happy note.
But thy eternal summer can no wrong do,
For no mortal for thy beauty may curse,
Nor pitiful Death through thy frame view
When above Time's trap dost thou course.
  This thy monument be—enthroned in men's eyes—
  For ages to see, and thy praise to arise.

INVISIBLE ADORATION

WHEN far removed from you,
Then do I with my most acute sense
Behold all the glorious wonders of your view,
Though Time ferries you farthest from hence.
For my eyes, like nascent stars in night's sky,
Who at dusk arise from their hole
Beneath the lie of heaven's eye,
Do paint the portrait of your whole to my soul.
They with short and long strokes, curvy and straight,
Draw faultless lines of your fair, and of your grace,
Saying in their hues, in your glare are too great,
And all of heaven's graces, do wholly embrace.
   What hap! That others in presence are seen best,
    But you, too beautiful, are in absence twice blest.

EPILOGUE

Poeta, Poeta, have you not read the paper,

Heard the whispers, rumors of your murder?

You've warred with power, rattled the tail of the viper,

Blared the sins of the monarch, like a crier.

Yes, 'tis true, I've wagered my soul for the stranger,

My peace for the pauper. *For love never fails, ever.*

Pelumi Olatinpo is a poet, a philosopher, a pioneer, a prophet of possibility, and a provocateur of our collective consciousness. A DREAMer and a technical startup founder, he sees our world for what it can be and not just what it is. An American-Nigerian, he lives in the Washington, D.C., area with his wife and two kids.